D1195947

Radio Control
Miniature Aircraft

Radio Control
Miniature Aircraft

ROBERT LOPSHIRE

MACMILLAN PUBLISHING CO., INC.

New York

COLLIER MACMILLAN PUBLISHERS

London

Copyright © 1974 by Macmillan Publishing Co., Inc.

Macmillan Publishing Co., Inc.
866 Third Avenue, New York, N.Y. 10022
Collier-Macmillan Canada Ltd.

Library of Congress Cataloging in Publication Data

Lopshire, Robert.
    Radio control miniature aircraft.

    1. Aeroplanes—Models—Radio control.   I. Title.
TL770.L57   1974b   629.133'1'34   73-7355
ISBN 0-02-575150-6

First Printing 1974

Printed in the United States of America

It is with genuine respect and admiration
that I dedicate this book to
DR. WALTER A. GOOD
on behalf of radio control
enthusiasts the world over.

PREFACE

The remote control of a device by means of radio transmission never fails to awe people, and it is no doubt this same awe that has led to your interest in getting to know more about radio control, or "R/C" as it is called by the thousands who enjoy this fascinating hobby or sport. R/C has something to offer all who take it up—young or old; male or female; laborer or executive—each devotee finds his particular slot in which to obtain hours of pleasure. As the newest hobby-sport in existence, it has a language all its own, a language that confuses the beginner and often makes him give up in frustration. The purpose of this book is to explain the language and "rules" in simple terms, hopefully saving you the often costly mistakes and frustrations that many beginners encounter. It is not a technical work in any sense; there are dozens of good technical books available on the subject, and the various modeling publications, with their ability to keep pace with the fast changes in technology, offer the reader the latest word monthly. This is only to get you started.

R/C planes can travel at very high speeds and involve use of potentially dangerous chemicals. Therefore anyone flying or building them must exercise skill and caution to avoid killing or seriously injuring himself or others. Fliers should also become thoroughly familiar with applicable laws and regulations before using radio frequencies or flying their planes.

CONTENTS

1

The Beginning of a Great Hobby

About 1935 two brothers named Good, who were amateur model airplane enthusiasts, built and successfully flew a model plane which was remotely controlled by a radio transmitter and receiver. This, insofar as can be determined, was the first radio-controlled flight ever made.

(*Fundamental Principles of Guided Missiles*, Volume 1. Guided Missile Structures Extension Course Institute, USAF, Air University.)

Their first plane, "Guff," now on permanent display at the Smithsonian in Washington, began life as a free-flight model in the style of the day—big! Built in 1935, "Guff" had an 8-foot wingspan, but surprisingly enough the weight was comparable to the average radio ship today, 8½ pounds when the radio equipment was installed a year later. Walter, the model builder, and William, a ham radio operator, built the plane and radio equipment as a class project while enrolled at Kalamazoo College, and exhibited it at a science fair there in 1936. The twins graduated with degrees in physics in 1937, making their all-important first flight in May of the same year, then going on to win the new radio competition at the 1938, 1939, and 1940 National Model Airplane Championships.

The war canceled the Nationals until 1946, and when the Good brothers returned to national competition in 1947, they again set the pace as the ones to try to beat.

Just as the Wright brothers established basic rules of flying, this unique pair, through thorough research, established the basic rules of radio control, ones that still stand today, well over 30 years later.

In a three-part article in the old *Air Trails* magazine (November, December 1940; January 1941), the Good brothers said the following, still applicable today: "The present ship carries two controls, rudder and elevator. It is suggested, however, that a rudder control alone is an adequate beginning. Complications arising from two controls are apt to be discouraging." (Amen!) They also discussed the hazards of vibration and the importance of mounting the receiver with sponge to avoid it, and stressed that success came with repeated checking of equipment.

Their original radio had two frequencies, one for rudder and one for elevator control. The airborne receiver was in fact two receivers, one for each "channel" of information being sent by the large, ground-based transmitter. Later converted to battery power, the transmitter was originally powered by plugging into an outlet at the end of a long extension cord. Made in the days before the space program and the resultant miniaturization of components, the transmitter was roughly the size of a dozen of today's transmitters strapped together.

The airborne receivers, batteries, and actuators weighed a total of 2 pounds, in contrast to present units that weigh as little as 9.5 ounces, and while the Good radio received controls for two surfaces, today's sophisticated receivers handle up to six control functions. Another major difference is price then and now. The Good system, all homebuilt from various commercially available components, cost roughly $25. A single-channel system, comparable to their early unit in that an actuator is used to move the control surface, presently retails for around $60. The present-day radios are of course much smaller and a lot more reliable, but the basic principle remains unchanged from the Good brothers' developments of the late '30s.

Present-day actuators used in small planes weigh 2.5 ounces, *with* batteries, and are located in the fuselage midsection. The Good brothers' actuators (or "control") weighed 0.5 ounce, without the batteries, and were mounted, one each, inside the rudder and the elevator (see illustration on page 3).

The plane itself was typical of the day in size and construction, having, as mentioned previously, an 8-foot wingspan. One method used by the brothers might help today's beginner in radio control—they first perfected their plane as a free-flight ship, adding the radio only when they knew the plane would fly "hands-off." Construction is most easily understood by viewing the plans for the fuselage and subassemblies. A note of the depression years appears on the plans in the suggestion that a yardstick be used

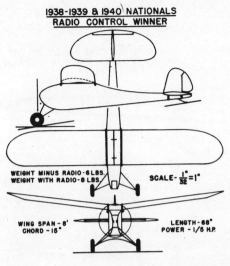

WEIGHT MINUS RADIO - 6 LBS.
WEIGHT WITH RADIO - 8 LBS.

SCALE - $\frac{1}{32}$" = 1"

WING SPAN - 8'
CHORD - 15"

LENGTH - 68"
POWER - 1/5 H.P.

Plans for the granddaddy of all radio controlled planes, Walter and William Good's "Guff." Note that the "controls," or actuators that moved the tail surfaces were mounted right in the surfaces.

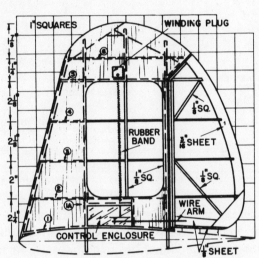

1" SQUARES

WINDING PLUG

RUBBER BAND

$\frac{1}{8}$" SQ.

$\frac{3}{16}$" SHEET

$\frac{1}{8}$" SQ.

WIRE ARM

$\frac{1}{8}$" SQ.

CONTROL ENCLOSURE

$\frac{1}{16}$" SHEET

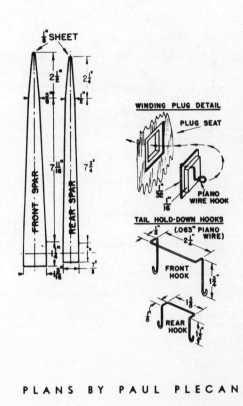

$\frac{1}{8}$" SHEET

2$\frac{1}{2}$"

2$\frac{1}{4}$"

FRONT SPAR

REAR SPAR

7$\frac{11}{16}$"

7$\frac{3}{4}$"

WINDING PLUG DETAIL

PLUG SEAT

PIANO WIRE HOOK

TAIL HOLD-DOWN HOOKS

(.063" PIANO WIRE)

FRONT HOOK

REAR HOOK

PLANS BY PAUL PLECAN

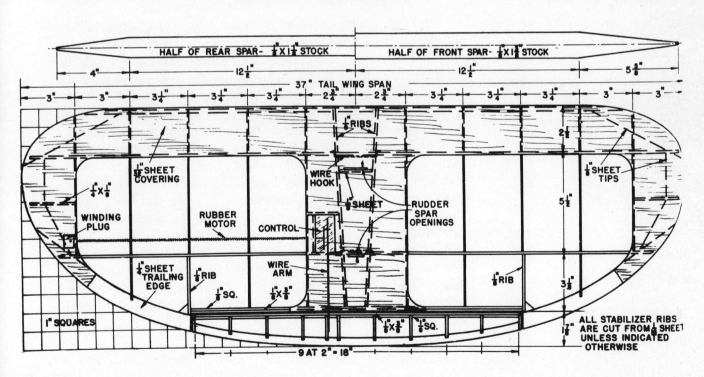

HALF OF REAR SPAR - $\frac{1}{4}$ X 1$\frac{1}{4}$ STOCK

HALF OF FRONT SPAR - $\frac{1}{4}$ X 1$\frac{1}{4}$ STOCK

4"

12$\frac{1}{2}$"

37" TAIL WING SPAN

12$\frac{1}{2}$"

5$\frac{3}{8}$"

3"

3"

3$\frac{1}{4}$"

3$\frac{1}{4}$"

3$\frac{1}{4}$"

2$\frac{3}{4}$"

2$\frac{3}{4}$"

3$\frac{1}{4}$"

3$\frac{1}{4}$"

3$\frac{1}{4}$"

3"

3"

$\frac{1}{8}$" RIBS

2$\frac{1}{2}$"

$\frac{1}{4}$ X $\frac{1}{8}$

WINDING PLUG

$\frac{1}{16}$" SHEET COVERING

RUBBER MOTOR

CONTROL

WIRE HOOK

$\frac{1}{8}$" SHEET

RUDDER SPAR OPENINGS

$\frac{1}{16}$" SHEET TIPS

5$\frac{1}{2}$"

$\frac{1}{16}$" SHEET TRAILING EDGE

$\frac{1}{8}$" RIB

$\frac{1}{8}$" SQ.

WIRE ARM

$\frac{1}{4}$ X $\frac{1}{8}$

$\frac{1}{8}$" RIB

3$\frac{1}{4}$"

$\frac{1}{4}$ X $\frac{1}{8}$

$\frac{1}{8}$" SQ.

1" SQUARES

9 AT 2" = 18"

1$\frac{1}{2}$"

ALL STABILIZER RIBS ARE CUT FROM $\frac{1}{8}$ SHEET UNLESS INDICATED OTHERWISE

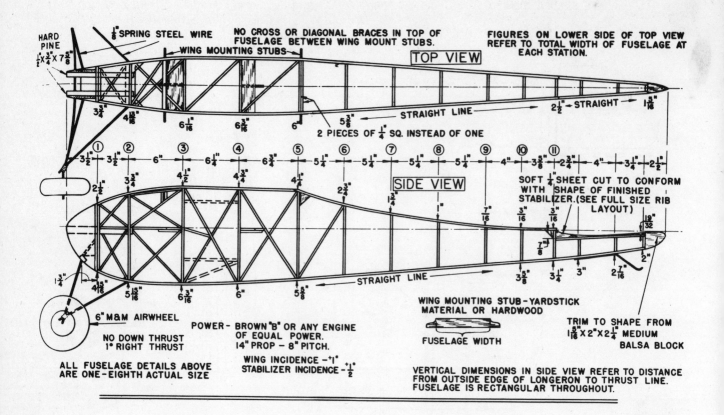

HARD PINE
1¼" X ¾" X 7⅞"

⅛" SPRING STEEL WIRE

WING MOUNTING STUBS

NO CROSS OR DIAGONAL BRACES IN TOP OF FUSELAGE BETWEEN WING MOUNT STUBS.

FIGURES ON LOWER SIDE OF TOP VIEW REFER TO TOTAL WIDTH OF FUSELAGE AT EACH STATION.

TOP VIEW

STRAIGHT LINE   2½" — STRAIGHT   1⅝"

2 PIECES OF ¼" SQ. INSTEAD OF ONE

3¾"   4⅝"   6¹⁄₁₆"   6¾"   6"   5⅝"

① 3½" ② 3½" 6" ③ 6¼" ④ 6¾" ⑤ 5¼" ⑥ 5¼" ⑦ 5¼" ⑧ 5¼" ⑨ 4" ⑩ 3⅝" ⑪ 2¾" 4" 3¼" 2½"

2½"   3¾"   4¼"   4¾"   4½"   2½"   1¼"   1"   ⁷⁄₁₆"   ³⁄₁₆"   ³⁄₁₆"

SIDE VIEW

SOFT ⅛" SHEET CUT TO CONFORM WITH SHAPE OF FINISHED STABILIZER. (SEE FULL SIZE RIB LAYOUT)

1⁹⁄₃₂"

1⅞"   4¹⁵⁄₁₆"   5¹³⁄₁₆"   6¾"   6"   5⅝"

⁷⁄₁₆"   2"

STRAIGHT LINE   3½"   3¼"   3"   2⁷⁄₁₆"

6" M&M AIRWHEEL

NO DOWN THRUST
1° RIGHT THRUST

POWER — BROWN "B" OR ANY ENGINE OF EQUAL POWER.
14" PROP — 8" PITCH.

WING INCIDENCE — +1°
STABILIZER INCIDENCE — -½°

WING MOUNTING STUB — YARDSTICK MATERIAL OR HARDWOOD

FUSELAGE WIDTH

TRIM TO SHAPE FROM 1⁵⁄₁₆" X 2" X 2½" MEDIUM BALSA BLOCK

ALL FUSELAGE DETAILS ABOVE ARE ONE-EIGHTH ACTUAL SIZE

VERTICAL DIMENSIONS IN SIDE VIEW REFER TO DISTANCE FROM OUTSIDE EDGE OF LONGERON TO THRUST LINE. FUSELAGE IS RECTANGULAR THROUGHOUT.

to make the wing-mounting stubs, but as you progress in radio control, you too will begin to see where one item, unrelated to modeling, can suddenly be just the required item for a specific use on a plane.

While your interest in radio control has no doubt been raised by seeing a plane put through wild aerobatics, the Good brothers, in 1940, recommended that the pilot concern himself with circles first, then a "figure eight," and finally the performance of flat spins, still perfect fare for today's beginner.

My first view of the Good brothers was in the early fifties when they appeared at a contest in southeastern Pennsylvania. The word spread like a brush fire in a wind: "They're here!" Everything stopped completely as every modeler on the field went to see this awesome pair fly their plane. In that time the experience was something like having the astronauts pay a visit to a function today. As the big transmitter was set up, the plane assembled, and the engine started, we stood like so many openmouthed schoolboys, nervously smiling at each other with the thought that we were to share this experience. The plane went up, circled lazily around, and came in to make a landing on the big concrete runway about a hundred feet away from the brothers. They could

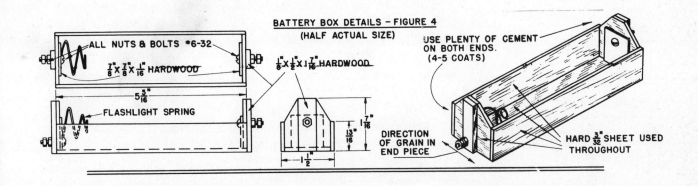

BATTERY BOX DETAILS – FIGURE 4
(HALF ACTUAL SIZE)

ALL NUTS & BOLTS #6-32

$\frac{7}{8}" \times \frac{7}{8}" \times \frac{1}{16}"$ HARDWOOD

$\frac{1}{8}" \times \frac{1}{2}" \times 1\frac{7}{16}"$ HARDWOOD

USE PLENTY OF CEMENT ON BOTH ENDS. (4-5 COATS)

$5\frac{5}{16}"$

FLASHLIGHT SPRING

$1\frac{7}{16}"$

$\frac{13}{16}"$

$1\frac{1}{2}"$

DIRECTION OF GRAIN IN END PIECE

HARD $\frac{3}{32}"$ SHEET USED THROUGHOUT

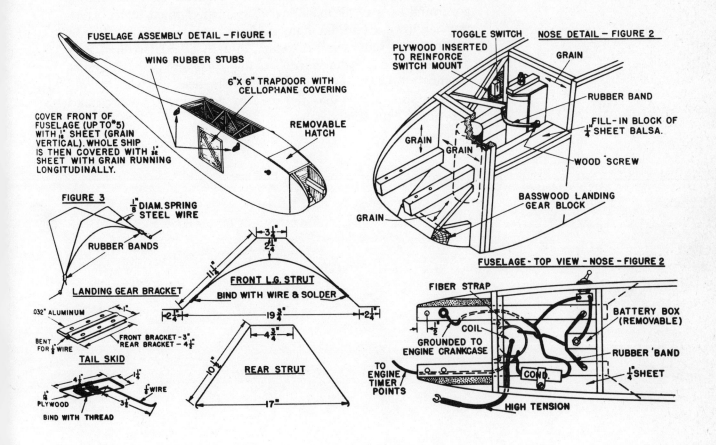

FUSELAGE ASSEMBLY DETAIL – FIGURE 1

WING RUBBER STUBS

6"X 6" TRAPDOOR WITH CELLOPHANE COVERING

REMOVABLE HATCH

COVER FRONT OF FUSELAGE (UP TO #5) WITH $\frac{1}{16}"$ SHEET (GRAIN VERTICAL). WHOLE SHIP IS THEN COVERED WITH $\frac{1}{32}"$ SHEET WITH GRAIN RUNNING LONGITUDINALLY.

FIGURE 3

$\frac{1}{8}"$ DIAM. SPRING STEEL WIRE

RUBBER BANDS

LANDING GEAR BRACKET

.032" ALUMINUM

BENT FOR $\frac{1}{8}"$ WIRE

FRONT BRACKET - 3"
REAR BRACKET - 4$\frac{1}{2}"$

TAIL SKID

PLYWOOD

$\frac{1}{4}"$ WIRE

BIND WITH THREAD

$3\frac{1}{4}"$

$3\frac{1}{4}"$
$2\frac{1}{4}"$

$11\frac{1}{2}"$

FRONT L.G. STRUT
BIND WITH WIRE & SOLDER

$2\frac{1}{4}"$

$19\frac{3}{4}"$

$2\frac{1}{4}"$

$4\frac{3}{4}"$

$10\frac{1}{2}"$

REAR STRUT

$17"$

NOSE DETAIL – FIGURE 2

TOGGLE SWITCH

PLYWOOD INSERTED TO REINFORCE SWITCH MOUNT

GRAIN

RUBBER BAND

FILL-IN BLOCK OF $\frac{1}{4}"$ SHEET BALSA.

GRAIN

GRAIN

WOOD SCREW

BASSWOOD LANDING GEAR BLOCK

GRAIN

FUSELAGE - TOP VIEW - NOSE - FIGURE 2

FIBER STRAP

BATTERY BOX (REMOVABLE)

$\frac{1}{2}"$

COIL

GROUNDED TO ENGINE CRANKCASE

RUBBER BAND

$\frac{1}{4}"$ SHEET

TO ENGINE TIMER POINTS

COND.

HIGH TENSION

have made the first successful moonshot. The applause was tremendous.

Where are the Good brothers today? Both are now doctors of physics. Dr. Walter Good resides in Bethesda, Maryland, and is a principal staff member of Johns Hopkins Applied Physics Laboratory in Silver Spring, Maryland. Dr. William Good, still a ham radio operator but no longer in modeling, is a research engineer with the General Electric Company at Electronics Park, Syracuse, New York. Walter, still an avid radio control enthusiast, was instrumental in the development of the proximity fuse and electronic fire control devices used in World War II.

Walter no longer builds his own radios. Like the average flyer, he uses commercially available units, and he builds from kits. He is a past president of the Academy of Model Aeronautics (AMA), governing body of all model aviation in the United States, is always on hand to run the monitors for a contest, is quite active in international radio control events, and is, at this writing, very much involved in radio control soaring. He is also probably one of the nicest people it has been my pleasure to meet, one who, in spite of his status, always has the time to share his knowledge and experience with others.

2
Some Points of Interest

While you've perhaps just discovered radio control, or R/C, as it will be referred to from here on, it may come as a surprise to you to know that R/C has been around since 1924 and that many of the things you take for granted also work on radio signals, much like the models you've seen or heard of.

For example, many cities control their stoplights by radio control from a central location. (In Europe police carry hand-held transmitters to change the stoplights as they wish.) There are military fighters flying over the United States in the company of a larger plane—with no pilot in the fighter. The pilot is in the larger plane, flying the fighter by means of a highly elaborate R/C system. Factories use R/C to send delivery and pick-up carts around with parts; hospitals have food carts going from kitchens into elevators and to points on each floor to deliver meals for patients; garage doors are opened and closed from cars by small R/C transmitters; and railroads use R/C to speed switching of cars at junctions.

While your interest will be in the use of R/C as applied to modeling, it is fascinating to look briefly at these other uses of R/C and realize how and where it has been used. In 1924 U.S. Navy experimenters flew a radio-controlled full-size seaplane, putting it through all sorts of maneuvers—until it crashed (a problem still plaguing beginners). In 1936 the Navy tried again, with success, and the N2C2 began a long career as a test bed for future developments, including target tracking practice for the gun crews of the U.S.S. *Ranger*. By the time World War II began, every large nation in the world had radio-controlled planes, and with the advent of the war, technology leaped ahead. The Germans developed R/C tanks that allowed the driver to approach a target, get out, send the tank ahead by radio control to drop its time charge, call the tank back, and get in and drive away.

People often ask how far a radio-controlled plane can fly, a matter we'll get to later; but in 1947, while hobbyists were struggling with homemade equipment of the crudest form, the U.S. Air Force flew a radio-controlled transport plane with no one aboard, to Great Britain and back to the United States!

Today's applications of R/C by the military are many, and while a great number are classified secrets, they range from the testing of full-size planes in flight to radio-controlled planes used as targets for missiles. Also used by the military and NASA are model planes, R/C directed, to fly into forest fires for heat studies, to test reentry vehicles, to test full-size aircraft designs before prototypes are constructed, and for a multitude of other money-saving uses.

You might wonder, with all these devices being controlled by radio waves, if the radio signals ever overlap and cause a device in one location to receive a signal meant for another. Radio frequencies, or precise broadcast, are very carefully allotted and monitored by the Federal Communications Commission (FCC) in the United States and similar bodies in other countries. In time of war, nations can "jam," or intercept and destroy, others' radio transmissions, but in peacetime the interference is relatively negligible and radio frequencies are assigned and carefully monitored to avoid problems.

Until the last few years, the R/C enthusiast, however, was plagued with interference problems unless he was a "ham" radio operator who operated his model's radio on the 6-meter band. Then the FCC allocated one segment of the radio band to what became known as "Citizens' Band Radio" (CB), with a group of frequencies around 27.000 megaHertz (mHz), formerly megacycles or mc. With a nontechnical, minimal license required, modelers rushed to use the band—and so did millions of Americans who put two-way radios in their cars on the same frequencies as the hobbyists. The radios used at the time were rather broad in their reception. Called "super-regenerative," they accepted information not necessarily meant for them. So it was that a modeler flying a plane at 300 feet on 26.995 mHz, would watch in horror as he suddenly saw his plane make an uncalled-for turn and corkscrew into the ground. Someone had picked up the microphone of his car radio and called his wife to see if dinner was ready, knocking several hundred dollars worth of equipment and many hours of work out of the sky and into pulverized junk. The term for this was "shot down," and it was caused by the "splatter," or inaccuracy, of much of the easily available citizen's band equipment and by the tinkerers who came along to play both with the crystals that determined the frequency of the transmitter and receiver and with the power supply. Americans love big numbers, and while most of the two-way radio systems left the factory with a more than adequate 5-watt power rating, many of the sets wound up converted to absurd power outputs.

The government finally realized it had created a monster in allowing "radio for all," and began to clamp down. The old license fee for such operation was raised from $8 every five years, to $20 every five years in an attempt to discourage a larger spread of the personal broadcasting systems. While many doubt that this will do much good to discourage the traveling blabbers, it is at least a step forward, and that, coupled with some very decisive action taken by the Academy of Model Aeronautics, has brightened the picture for the hobbyist immensely.

Until very recently, the super-regenerative radio was by and large the *only* radio hobbyists used. The more precise superheterodyne radios were heavier and more expensive, and along with the radios in cars that seemed to be on at all times, there were those earlier mentioned traffic light control systems on the same frequencies. The light control system in Los Angeles became grudgingly known as "King Kong" by flyers in that area. With the lights changing every few minutes, one had to be brave indeed to try a flight. King Kong was seemingly as fatal as the Luftwaffe, albeit in miniature. Then products from the space age began to drift down for use by the common man. Along came the tiny transistor: printed circuits replaced bulky wiring, and precision and reliability replaced guesswork and "maybe." Hobbyists with electronic training began to manufacture radio sets, and the new lightweight "superheterodyne" radios emerged to transmit and receive extremely precise radio signals. Gone was the guesswork; here was the reliability that had seemingly taken ages to achieve. (Watching one's pride and joy scream into the earth to demolish itself may take but five seconds. It always seemed like five years, and aged the enthusiast an equal amount of time.)

Then the Academy of Model Aeronautics after meager beginnings in the mid-'30s, having grown into the biggest modeling organization in the world by the mid-'60s, entered the picture to lobby for legislation for modelers. Obtaining legal counsel who appeared frequently before the FCC (and still does), the AMA obtained certain set frequencies specifically allotted for the use of modelers on the grounds that modeling and radio control were a very important part of this country's development in the field of advanced technology. Almost every single astronaut had his beginnings in modeling, and with astronauts as national heroes, who could deny that modeling was not something to be taken seriously, and that the AMA should perhaps be listened to?

So it was that 17 specific radio frequencies were set aside for the use of modeling by the FCC. Even though some are shared in a sense by other radio users, the new superheterodyne systems pretty well establish the frequencies as ones being interference-free in most respects. These are:

> 6 Meter, or Ham Band—52.950 mHz, 53.100 mHz, 53.200 mHz, 53.300 mHz, and 53.500 mHz. To use any of these frequencies for transmission of radio signals, one *must* be a fully licensed amateur radio operator, meeting all FCC requirements.

> Citizens' Band—26.995 mHz, 27.045 mHz, 27.095 mHz, 27.145 mHz, 27.195 mh. To use any of these frequencies, one must qualify under the citizens' licensing as shown at the end of this chapter.

> Citizens' Band, Model Use Only—72.080 mHz, 72.160 mHz, 72.240 mHz, 72.320 mHz, 72.400 mHz, 72.960 mHz, 75.640 mHz. To use any of these frequencies one must qualify under the citizens' licensing as shown at the end of this chapter.

So that you may now have your first lesson in the language of R/C, the term "6 meters" means that the measured transmitted length of a radio signal, or "wave," is precisely 6 meters or 19.6805 feet (at 39.37 inches a meter). If you imagine waves washing ashore in an ocean, you can then imagine that the radio "waves" are spaced precisely 19.6805 feet apart from crest to crest as they approach the receiver from the transmitter. All radio signals are sent forth from transmitter to receiver in a like fashion, and the precise measurement of the waves crest to crest, determines the wave length.

Therefore, the next thing to consider is the frequency with which these precisely spaced waves approach the receiver from the transmitter. If a receiver and transmitter are said to be on 53.100 mHz, then each second 53.100 million waves go from transmitter to receiver. Flying at the same time, another R/C enthusiast can use a transmitter that sends forth 53.200 million radio waves a second, and not interfere with the flyer sending 53.100. While this may seem to be a very slim margin, it is wide indeed in the precisely measured world of electronics.

Today the 27-mHz group of frequencies is seldom the victim of interference. Government regulations finally put the car-borne radios on frequencies of 26.62, 27.575, and 27.585 mHz, all far enough away from 26.995 through 27.195 to avoid problems for the modeler. There are rare occasions of interference for the R/C hobbyist, but they are mostly caused by other R/C'ers who may be using their transmitters in a nearby area. For this reason one should scout the surrounding countryside to see if there is a flying field, boat basin, or car track for R/C before operating one's own equipment in what may seem to be an ideal location.

The 72-mHz frequencies are the result of AMA effort to obtain frequencies for model use alone. This group of frequencies has become very popular for use with gliders because a glider can stay up for a very long time, and, with no chance of interference, one can relax and enjoy the flight without worry. In crowded areas, or places where contests are being held, clubs normally set up a monitoring system to keep an eye on frequencies being used on and off the field. If strange signals suddenly appear on the frequency being flown, the flyer is notified immediately so that he may land his plane at once.

27 mhz

72 mhz

53 mhz

FREQUENCY RACK

Flying field frequency rack. Clothespins, painted with the various color combinations of individual frequencies, are removed by a flyer and placed on his transmitter antenna when he wishes to fly. Anyone else on the same frequency, seeing that the pin of his color is not on the rack, keeps his transmitter turned off until the pin is returned to the rack. This system, when respected by all flyers, avoids any possible "shoot downs" of airborne planes.

While the government has placed, for the good of all, restrictions on the frequencies and how they are used, AMA and AMA clubs have also established many safety rules, without which there would be utter chaos at contests and weekly fly-for-fun sessions. Transmitters are impounded until it is a flyer's turn to take to the air at contests, and almost all clubs now use the "safety pin" method on their club fields. The safety pin system is one where 17 clothespins are painted with the 17 colors and color combinations that have been assigned to the 17 model use frequencies. If a flyer wishes to send his plane aloft, he first checks either with the club safety officer who hands out the pins, or he checks the "pin-rack" (see page 11) to see if his frequency is in use. If he is, for example, flying on 72.960, his color pin will be yellow and white. If the yellow and white pin is not on the rack it means someone else is using that frequency. If the pin is on the rack, the flyer takes it and clamps it on his transmitter's antenna, returning it to the rack when his flight is completed. This system, when used and respected by all, allows a smooth-running afternoon of flying with no risk of interference. However, a flyer still has to remember not to turn on his transmitter to check a control function, unless he has the color-coded pin. To do so means instant trouble for anyone who might be flying on the same frequency at the moment. The following is a listing of frequencies and their color codes:

27 mHz			53 mHz			72 mHz	
26.995	Brown		53.10	Brown & Black		72.08	Brown & White
27.045	Red		53.20	Red & Black		72.16	Light Blue & White
27.095	Orange		53.30	Orange & Black		72.24	Red & White
27.145	Yellow		53.40	Yellow & Black		72.32	Violet & White
27.195	Green		53.50	Green & Black		72.40	Orange & White
27.225	Blue					72.96	Yellow & White
						75.64	Green & White

While on the subject of clubs and their means of insuring interference-free operations, there are other advantages to membership in a club for a beginner. While individuals working alone are often successful in controlling their first boat or radio, the novice *flyer* seldom is. While the boat and car work upon a surface, only able to go right or left, the airplane is free to go up and down as well. If a boat gets into trouble from faulty installation of radio equipment it may require some rowing or swimming to retrieve it, but nothing is harmed. The car may crash into a curb or other obstruction, but the damage will usually be minor. The airplane, however, engine howling, is quite a different story when things go wrong, and the end results are normally not worth taking home.

By joining a club, and/or asking the members for help, the beginner can save himself countless hours of mistakes and frustration. Beginning with questions as to what radio equipment, what kit, what engine he needs, and so on, the beginner can be off to a good start based on the knowledge of experienced flyers. As construction progresses on the first plane, any difficulties encountered can be overcome quickly by asking for help among the club members, most of whom are usually quite glad to be of aid.

When it comes time for the first flight, it is always best to have an experienced flyer on hand to check out the plane beforehand, and to assist with the flying itself. The beginner tends to overcontrol a model, the result being that once the plane gets into a critical attitude, the over-control sends it careening into yet another crisis. One of our most famous astronauts, who shall remain nameless, took up R/C and, when offered help, turned it down to go make his first flights by himself. With thousands of hours of flying time, he figured that if anyone could handle a R/C plane he could. You guessed it—he piled the plane in shortly after takeoff, and went home a sadder but wiser astronaut.

While the flying of R/C planes does not require super talent, it does require some instruction and help in the beginning. Experience in a full-size plane means nothing when one picks up the transmitter to send his model skyward. When seated in an airplane, one is able to apply control, feel it take effect, and give more or less control as needed. Flying by remote control allows for no "seat of the pants" flying. It is a skill all of its own, best acquired under the watchful supervision of an experienced instructor.

Aside from flying skills to be acquired with the aid of an experienced flyer, the beginner will also begin to gain other skills as a benefit of club membership. Clubs are seldom composed of people with but one interest in R/C, but rather of those who wish only to fly, those who love to build, those whose love is radio, and so on. The beginner will soon find his particular slot and advance rapidly with the aid of those in the club who have the same interest.

So, while this book is designed to get the beginner over a number of hurdles, the advice on joining a club still stands. To obtain the name of a club near you, drop a line to the Academy of Model Aeronautics, 806 15th St., N.W., Washington, D.C. 20005.

Radio Control World Records
(As of September, 1973)

Aeroplane, Duration	M. HIROTA, Japan	12h 43m 2s
Aeroplane, Distance	A. BELLOCCHINO, Italy	243.7 mi.
Aeroplane, Height	M. HILL, USA	26,919 ft.
Aeroplane, Speed	GOUKOUN AND MYAKININ, USSR	213.7 mph.
Aeroplane, Distance*	B. D. KUNCE, USA	210.04 mi.
Glider, Duration	E. M. CIRRUS, Norway	19h 19m 9s
Glider, Distance	J. KRAINOCK, W. Ger.	18.44 mi.
Glider, Height	RAY SMITH, USA	4,988 ft.
Glider, Speed	L. ALDOCHINE, USSR	113.24 mph.
Glider, Distance*	M. SMITH, USA	284.6 mi.
HC,† Duration	M. KUFNER, W. Ger.	1h 12m 23.5s
HC, Distance	ABRAGEEV, USSR	6,043 ft.
HC, Height	E. ROCK, USA	649.6 ft.
HC, Speed	No Record Established	
HC, Distance*	J. BITTERER, W. Ger.	9.33 mi.
Seaplane, Duration	W. K. FED, E. Ger.	6h 18m 17s
Seaplane, Distance	R. D. REED, USA	83.186 mi.
Seaplane, Height	M. HILL, USA	18,540 ft.
Seaplane, Speed	GOUKOUN & MYAKININ, USSR	183.29 mph.
Seaplane, Distance*	W. KAISER, W. Ger.	148.41 mi.

* Over a closed course
† HC stands for Helicopter

FCC FORM 505
– JULY 1970

UNITED STATES OF AMERICA
FEDERAL COMMUNICATIONS COMMISSION
WASHINGTON, D.C. 20554
APPLICATION FOR CLASS B, C, OR D STATION LICENSE IN THE

FORM APPROVED
BUDGET BUREAU NO. 52–R0123

CITIZENS RADIO SERVICE

1. Application for Class A station license must be filed on FCC FORM 400.
2. Complete on typewriter or print clearly.
3. Be sure application is signed and dated. *Mail* application to Federal Communications Commission, Gettysburg, Pa. 17325.
4. Enclose appropriate fee with application, DO NOT SUBMIT CASH. Make check or money order payable to Federal Communications Commission. THE FEE WILL NOT BE REFUNDED EVEN IF THE APPLICATION IS NOT GRANTED. Also, fee overpayments of $2 or less will not be refunded. (No fee is required for an application filed by a governmental entity. For additional fee details, including exemptions, see Subpart G of Part I of the Commission's Rules.) READ INSTRUCTIONS FOR EACH ITEM BEFORE FILLING IN THE APPLICATION—TYPE OR PRINT.

DO NOT WRITE IN THIS BLOCK

1 (a) NAME OF APPLICANT

BUSINESS NAME (*if any*) OR, IF APPLYING AS AN INDIVIDUAL, GIVE LAST NAME

FIRST NAME (*if an individual*) — MIDDLE INITIAL

1 (b) PERMANENT MAILING ADDRESS
NUMBER   STREET

CITY   STATE   ZIP CODE

COUNTY:

1 (c) BIRTHPLACE AND DATE (See Instruction (c))

CITY	STATE	MONTH	DAY	YEAR

1 (d) IF APPLICANT IS AN INDIVIDUAL/DBA (See Item 4), INSERT TRADE NAME OR BUSINESS NAME

2 NAMES OF PARTNERS (*Do not repeat any name shown in Item 1*)

(a) LAST NAME	FIRST NAME	MIDDLE INITIAL

2 (b) BIRTHPLACE AND DATE (See Instruction (c))

CITY	STATE	MONTH	DAY	YEAR

3 IF ITEM 1 SHOWS P.O. BOX OR RFD NUMBER, GIVE A LOCATION WHERE THE LICENSEE OR THE STATION MAY BE FOUND. (*Do not give post office box or RFD number.*)

NUMBER AND STREET

CITY   STATE

IF LOCATION CANNOT BE SPECIFIED BY STREET, CITY, AND STATE, GIVE OTHER DESCRIPTION OF LOCATION SUCH AS DISTANCE AND DIRECTION FROM NEAREST MAJOR ROAD INTERSECTION OR FROM NEAREST TOWN OR CITY.

4 CLASSIFICATION OF APPLICANT (*See Instructions*)

☐ INDIVIDUAL   ☐ ASSOCIATION   ☐ GOVERNMENTAL ENTITY

☐ INDIVIDUAL/DBA   ☐ CORPORATION   ☐ OTHER (*Specify*)

☐ BUSINESS PARTNERSHIP

5 CLASS OF STATION (*Check only one*) (*See Instruction 5*)

☐ CLASS B   ☐ CLASS C (NON-VOICE TRANSMITTER)   ☐ CLASS D (VOICE)

6 IS THIS APPLICATION TO MODIFY OR RENEW AN EXISTING STATION LICENSE?

☐ YES (*Give call sign*):   ☐ NO

7 DO YOU NOW HOLD ANY STATION LICENSE, OTHER THAN THAT COVERED BY ITEM 6, OF THE SAME CLASS AS THAT REQUESTED BY THIS APPLICATION? (*See Instruction 7*)

☐ YES   ☐ NO

IF "YES", FURNISH CALL SIGN(S)

8 NUMBER OF TRANSMITTERS (*give the total number of transmitters expected to be operated during the next 5 years*)

NUMBER

ATTACH STATEMENT GIVING PROPOSED LOCATION AND USE OF TRANSMITTERS WHEN:
  a. APPLICANT PROPOSES MORE THAN 3 TRANSMITTERS FOR CLASS C USE.
  b. AN INDIVIDUAL APPLICANT PROPOSES MORE THAN 6 TRANSMITTERS.
  c. THE CLASSIFICATION OF APPLICANT (*Item 4*) IS OTHER THAN INDIVIDUAL AND APPLICATION SPECIFIES MORE THAN 12 TRANSMITTERS.

CHECK APPROPRIATE BOXES	YES	NO
9 (a) IS EACH TRANSMITTER TO BE OPERATED AS A CLASS D STATION, OR AS A CLASS C STATION IN THE 72–76 MC/S BAND, TYPE APPROVED OR TYPE ACCEPTED BY THE COMMISSION?		
(b) IS EACH TRANSMITTER TO BE OPERATED IN THE 26–27 MC/S BAND CRYSTAL CONTROLLED? (*If you have checked "NO" to both (a) and (b), attach detailed description: See Subpart C of Part 95.*)		
10 (a) WILL APPLICANT OWN ALL THE RADIO EQUIPMENT? (*If "NO", answer (b) and (c) below*)		
(b) NAME OF OWNER		
(c) IF NOT THE OWNER OF THE RADIO EQUIPMENT, IS APPLICANT A PARTY TO A LEASE OR OTHER AGREEMENT UNDER WHICH CONTROL WILL BE EXERCISED IN THE SAME MANNER AS IF THE EQUIPMENT WERE OWNED BY THE APPLICANT?		
11 HAS APPLICANT READ AND UNDERSTOOD THE PROVISIONS OF PART 95, DEALING WITH PROHIBITED COMMUNICATIONS AND USES?		
12 DOES THE APPLICANT CERTIFY THAT THE STATION WILL NOT BE USED FOR RADIOTELEPHONE COMMUNICATION OVER A DISTANCE EXCEEDING 150 MILES, OR FOR THE EXCHANGE OF CHIT-CHAT, IDLE CONVERSATION, DISCUSSION OF EQUIPMENT, OR HOBBY-TYPE COMMUNICATIONS?		
13 WILL ANY PERSON, OTHER THAN (1) THE APPLICANT, (2) MEMBERS OF HIS IMMEDIATE FAMILY LIVING IN THE SAME HOUSEHOLD, OR (3) HIS EMPLOYEES, OPERATE THE STATION? (*If "YES", attach a separate sheet listing the names and relationship of all such persons and give a detailed reason for their operation of your station*)		
14 IF APPLICANT IS AN INDIVIDUAL OR A PARTNERSHIP, ARE YOU OR ANY OF THE PARTNERS AN ALIEN? (*If the answer is "YES", do not file this application because you are not eligible for a license*)		
15 IS APPLICANT THE REPRESENTATIVE OF ANY ALIEN OR OF ANY FOREIGN GOVERNMENT? (*If "YES", explain under Remarks on the reverse side*)		
16 WITHIN 10 YEARS PREVIOUS TO THE DATE OF THIS APPLICATION, HAS THE APPLICANT OR ANY PARTY TO THIS APPLICATION BEEN CONVICTED IN A FEDERAL, STATE OR LOCAL COURT OF ANY CRIME FOR WHICH THE PENALTY IMPOSED WAS A FINE OF $500 OR MORE, OR AN IMPRISONMENT OF 6 MONTHS OR MORE? (*If "YES", see Instruction 16*)		
17 IF APPLICANT IS AN INDIVIDUAL OR A PARTNERSHIP, ARE YOU OR ANY PARTNER LESS THAN 18 YEARS OF AGE (LESS THAN 12 YEARS OF AGE IF FOR CLASS C STATION LICENSE)? (*If the answer is "YES", do not file this application. Persons under 18 are not eligible for a Class D license and persons under 12 are not eligible for a Class C license*)		

18   RESERVED

				DO NOT WRITE IN THIS BOX
SCREENING	☐ Y	☐ N		
SIGNATURE	☐ Y	☐ N		

SIGN AND DATE THE APPLICATION ON REVERSE SIDE

GENERAL INFORMATION AND INSTRUCTIONS

DO NOT OPERATE YOUR TRANSMITTER UNTIL YOU HAVE BEEN ISSUED A LICENSE BY THE COMMISSION. THE USE OF ANY CALL SIGN NOT YOUR OWN IS PROHIBITED. THE COMMUNICATIONS ACT OF 1934 PROVIDES SEVERE PENALTIES FOR UNLICENSED OPERATION.

YOUR APPLICATION WILL BE PROCESSED AS SOON AS POSSIBLE IN THE ORDER OF ITS RECEIPT BY THE COMMISSION. DO NOT TELEPHONE THE COMMISSION'S OFFICE IN GETTYSBURG, PA., CONCERNING THE STATUS OF PENDING APPLICATIONS OR OTHER INFORMATION RELATING TO THE CITIZENS RADIO SERVICE. THE GETTYSBURG OFFICE IS NOT EQUIPPED TO ANSWER TELEPHONE INQUIRIES. ANY INQUIRIES CONCERNING APPLICATIONS PENDING MORE THAN 6 WEEKS SHOULD BE DIRECTED, PREFERABLY IN WRITING, TO THE COMMISSION'S OFFICE IN WASHINGTON, D.C. 20554. THE INCLUSION OF POSTAGE STAMPS IS UNNECESSARY AND WILL ONLY DELAY PROCESSING.

Applicant must have a current copy of Federal Communications Commission Rules and Regulations, Volume VI, Part 95, "Citizens Radio Service." (See the order blank above.) *Checks or money orders for copies of the Commission's Rules must be made payable to Superintendent of Documents and mailed directly to Government Printing Office, Washington, D.C. 20402.*

Detach and fill out the "Work Sheet" with a pencil or on a typewriter as you desire. When you are satisfied that you have all the required information written correctly on the "Work Sheet," copy this data on the application form itself with a typewriter or print clearly. Keep the "Work Sheet" for your file copy and send the completed application to the Federal Communications Commission, Gettysburg, Pa., 17325.

Be sure to include all details of the station to be operated under this license. When the license is issued it will be your sole operating authority for the class of station applied for and will supersede any previous authorization for the same class.

Read and answer all questions carefully. Your signature certifies that the statements you have made are true. ANY WILLFUL FALSE STATEMENTS MADE ON THIS FORM ARE PUNISHABLE BY FINE AND IMPRISONMENT. U.S. CODE, TITLE 18, SECTION 1001.

DEFINITION

STATION—FOR THE PURPOSE OF THIS APPLICATION, A STATION INCLUDES ALL TRANSMITTERS AUTHORIZED UNDER A PARTICULAR LICENSE AND CALL SIGN.

SPECIFIC INSTRUCTIONS

ITEM 1(a)—If you are an INDIVIDUAL, insert your last name, first name and middle initial in that order. If you are an INDIVIDUAL doing business under a business or trade name (sole proprietorship), insert your name in Item 1(a) and the business or trade name in Item 1(d). If applicant is a married woman, use the given name in Item 1(a), such as Doe, Mary S. (not Doe, Mrs. John).

If applicant is a PARTNERSHIP doing business under a business or trade name, insert the trade name in Item 1(a) and the name of each partner in Item 2. If there is no trade name, enter name of one partner in Item 1(a) and the name(s) of all other partners in Item 2.

If applicant is a GOVERNMENTAL ENTITY, give the full legal name in Item 1(a) as stated in its authorization document; if a COR-

PORATION OR ASSOCIATION, give name in Item 1(a) exactly as it appears in the articles of incorporation or association.

ITEM 1(b)—Give *permanent mailing address;* DO NOT GIVE AN A.P.O. OR NAVY NUMBER OR AN OVERSEAS ADDRESS. Such addresses will result in rejection of the application. If license is desired to be mailed to such an address, so indicate under remarks.

ITEM 1(c)—Individual and partners must enter birth place and date on line opposite name in Item 1(c) or Item 2(b) as appropriate. Corporations, associations, and governmental entities need not supply this information.

ITEM 3—The information required in this space is a location at which the licensee or the station can be found by FCC personnel, if the permanent mailing address given under item 1(b) is indeterminate, such as a P.O. box or RFD number. If this location cannot be described by number and/or street, give other description such as "3 miles north of Waldorf on US 301." DO NOT GIVE POST OFFICE BOX OR RFD NUMBER. If a street and number or other specific location is given in item 1(b), do not repeat in item 3, but insert "same."

ITEM 4—Check only *one* box. If applicant is:

(a) An individual applying for personal or for business use without a trade name, check "INDIVIDUAL."
(b) An individual applying under a trade or business name, check "INDIVIDUAL/DBA." (DBA means Doing Business As.)
(c) A legal *business* partnership, check "BUSINESS PARTNERSHIP." A station license to a partnership may be used only for the business of that partnership and may not be used in connection with the personal activities of the partners.
(d) An unincorporated association, check "ASSOCIATION." See Section 95.13(b) for showing required.
(e) An incorporated association check "CORPORATION."
(f) A city, township, or other governmental body, check "GOVERNMENTAL ENTITY." Radio stations belonging to and operated by the United States Government cannot be licensed in the Citizens Radio Service.
(g) A trust or joint venture, check "OTHER," specify classification in space provided, and explain under Remarks. List joint venturers, and provide full information on each under items 19 or 20, if applicable.

ITEM 5—Check one box to indicate the class of station for which applying. A separate application is required for each class of station, as follows:

Class B—The Class B category of station is terminated as of November 1, 1971. Only applications for renewal of currently licensed stations will be accepted and any licenses issued will expire October 31, 1971.

Class C—Non-voice transmissions for the control by radio of remote objects or devices such as model airplanes, garage doors, etc. (Frequencies 26.995 to 27.255; also 72.08 to 75.64.) Please verify if class station checked is correct.

Class D—Voice operations only on frequencies 26.965 to 27.225 and 27.255. Please verify if class station checked is correct.

Applications for Citizens Class A Station Licenses must use FCC Form 400.

ITEM 7—Check one box. No person may hold more than one Class B, one Class C, and one Class D station license. Therefore, you should

CONTINUED ON REVERSE

19 IF APPLICANT IS A NONGOVERNMENTAL CORPORATION, ANSWER THE FOLLOWING ITEMS:	YES	NO
A IS CORPORATION ORGANIZED UNDER LAWS OF ANY FOREIGN GOVERNMENT? *(1) If Yes do not file the application because you are not eligible for a station license.*		
(2) If No, under the laws of what State is the corporation organized?		
B IS ANY OFFICER OR DIRECTOR OF THE CORPORATION AN ALIEN? *(If yes, do not file the application because you are not eligible for a station license)*		
C IS MORE THAN ONE-FIFTH OF THE CAPITAL STOCK EITHER OWNED OF RECORD OR MAY IT BE VOTED BY ALIENS OR THEIR REPRESENTATIVES, OR BY A FOREIGN GOVERNMENT OR REPRESENTATIVE THEREOF, OR BY ANY CORPORATION ORGANIZED UNDER THE LAWS OF A FOREIGN COUNTRY? *(If yes, do not file the application because you are not eligible for a station license)*		
D IS APPLICANT DIRECTLY OR INDIRECTLY CONTROLLED BY ANY OTHER CORPORATION? *(If yes, answer items E through K below)*		
E GIVE NAME AND ADDRESS OF CONTROLLING CORPORATION		
F UNDER THE LAWS OF WHAT STATE OR COUNTRY IS THE CONTROLLING CORPORATION ORGANIZED?		
G IS MORE THAN ONE-FOURTH OF THE CAPITAL STOCK OF CONTROLLING CORPORATION EITHER OWNED OF RECORD OR MAY IT BE VOTED BY ALIENS OR THEIR REPRESENTATIVES, OR BY A FOREIGN GOVERNMENT OR REPRESENTATIVE THEREOF, OR BY ANY CORPORATION ORGANIZED UNDER THE LAWS OF A FOREIGN COUNTRY? *(If yes, give details)*		
H IS ANY OFFICER OR MORE THAN ONE-FOURTH OF THE DIRECTORS OF THE CONTROLLING CORPORATION AN ALIEN? *(If yes, answer items I and J below)*		
I TOTAL NUMBER OF DIRECTORS IN CONTROLLING CORPORATION		
J LIST THE NAME, NATIONALITY AND OFFICE HELD FOR ALL OFFICERS AND DIRECTORS WHO ARE ALIENS IN CONTROLLING CORPORATION AND GIVE BRIEF BIOGRAPHICAL STATEMENT FOR EACH ALIEN ON A SEPARATE SHEET OF PAPER.		
K IS THE CONTROLLING CORPORATION IN TURN CONTROLLED BY OTHER COMPANIES? *(If yes, attach information for each of these controlling companies covering the information requested in items E through K)*	☐ YES ☐ NO	

20 IF APPLICANT IS AN UNINCORPORATED ASSOCIATION, ANSWER THE FOLLOWING ITEMS:	YES	NO
A IS ANY OFFICER OR DIRECTOR OF THE ASSOCIATION AN ALIEN? *(If yes, do not file the application because you are not eligible for a station license)*		
B ARE MORE THAN ONE-FIFTH OF THE VOTING MEMBERS OF THE ASSOCIATION ALIENS OR REPRESENTATIVES OF ALIENS, FOREIGN GOVERNMENTS OR REPRESENTATIVES THEREOF, OR CORPORATIONS ORGANIZED UNDER THE LAWS OF A FOREIGN COUNTRY? *(If yes, do not file the application because you are not eligible for a station license)*		
C IS THE ASSOCIATION DIRECTLY OR INDIRECTLY CONTROLLED BY ANY OTHER ORGANIZATION? *(If yes, give detailed explanation)*		

USE THIS SPACE FOR ANY ADDITIONAL INFORMATION OR REMARKS

WILLFUL FALSE STATEMENTS MADE ON THIS FORM ARE PUNISHABLE BY FINE AND IMPRISONMENT. U.S. CODE, TITLE 18, SECTION 1001.

ALL THE STATEMENTS MADE IN THE APPLICATION AND ATTACHED EXHIBITS ARE CONSIDERED MATERIAL REPRESENTATIONS, AND ALL THE EXHIBITS ARE A MATERIAL PART HEREOF AND ARE INCORPORATED HEREIN AS IF SET OUT IN FULL IN THE APPLICATION.

I CERTIFY THAT:

The applicant has (or has ordered from the Government Printing Office) a current copy of Part 95 of the Commission's rules governing the Citizens Radio Service;

The applicant waives any claim to the use of any particular frequency or of the ether as against the regulatory power of the United States because of the previous use of the same, whether by license or otherwise;

The applicant accepts full responsibility for the operation of, and will retain control of any citizens radio station licensed to him pursuant to this application;

The station will be operated in full accordance with the applicable law and the current rules of the Federal Communications Commission;

The said station will not be used for any purpose contrary to Federal, State or local law;

The applicant will have unlimited access to the radio equipment and effective measures will be taken to prevent its use by unauthorized persons; and

The statements in this application are true, complete, and correct to the best of my knowledge and belief and are made in good faith.

SIGNATURE: _____ DATE SIGNED: _____

(Check appropriate box below):

☐ INDIVIDUAL APPLICANT ☐ MEMBER OF APPLICANT PARTNERSHIP ☐ OFFICER OF APPLICANT CORPORATION ☐ OFFICER WHO IS ALSO A MEMBER OF THE APPLICANT ASSOCIATION ☐ OFFICIAL OF GOVERNMENTAL ENTITY not apply for an additional station license of a class you already hold. Instead, you may apply for modification of your present license(s), if any, to include all transmitters you expect to operate under each class during a 5-year term. Class B, C, and D stations may be operated anywhere in the United States.

ITEM 9—If you are applying for a Class C station license using frequencies in the 72–76 Mc/s band, the transmitting equipment you propose to use must either be on the Commission's "Radio Equipment List," or you must attach a complete description of your transmitter in accordance with Subpart C of Part 95 of the Rules. If you are applying for a Class C station license using frequencies in the 26–27 Mc/s band or a Class D station license, the transmitting equipment must either be crystal-controlled or must appear on the above-mentioned list. If not, you must attach a complete description as indicated above.

ITEM 12—This item is your certification as to whether or not the use of the station for which authorization is requested will conform at all times with the permissible communications set forth in the Commission's rules, including the prohibitions against nonsubstantive and "skip" communications. The 150-mile limit on communications has been used for convenience but reflects the requirement that communications be directed to stations within the direct groundwave coverage range. Groundwave communications of 150 miles are far beyond the normal capability of citizens radio stations, and "skip" or "skywave" communications may not be expected to occur except at distances considerably greater than that.

ITEM 16—This question need not be answered by applicants which are governmental entities nor by the officials signing on behalf of such governmental entities. In all other cases the question must be answered "Yes" or "No" as appropriate. The words "applicant or any party to this application" have the following meanings, respectively:

(1) In case of an individual applicant, the applicant.
(2) In case of a partnership applicant, any partners, including general, limited (special), and silent (dormant) partners.
(3) In case of a joint venture applicant, any joint venturers.
(4) In case of a corporate applicant or a corporate joint venturer, the corporation itself or any officers or directors.

(5) In case of an unincorporated association applicant or an unincorporated association joint venturer, any executive officers or members of the governing board.

If the question is answered "Yes," furnish the following information:
(1) For *each* such conviction, give these details—
    (a) The name of the person convicted and his relationship to applicant. (For example, "applicant," "director of corporate applicant.")
    (b) The nature of the offense, the date of the conviction, and the name and address of the court.
    (c) The sentence imposed, including the fine and imprisonment. If execution of the sentence was suspended in whole or in part, state to what extent it was suspended.
    (d) The dates of commencement and termination of actual imprisonment, if any.
    (e) If released on parole, give the dates of commencement and termination of parole, and state whether or not parole was successfully completed without incident. If presently on parole, give name and address of parole officer.
    (f) State whether or not radio facilities were used in committing the offense. If such facilities were so used, describe how they were used.
(2) With reference to the person convicted, a statement as to the nature and duration of his present employment or business activity, and the name and address of his employer.
(3) A description of the proposed use of Citizens Radio if the requested license were to be issued..

ITEM 17—Self-explanatory.

ITEM 19—To be completed by those applicants classified as "corporation."

ITEM 20—To be completed by those applicants classified as "association."

CERTIFICATION AND SIGNATURE—Application is not complete unless signed and dated. If the applicant is a corporation, the signature must be that of an officer. If applicant is an association, the signature must be that of a member who is an officer. If applicant is a partnership, the signature must be that of a responsible partner.

3
Getting Started

It seems that one of the first questions asked by people seeing for the first time a miniature plane, car, or boat controlled by radio is, "How much does it cost?" A simple question, but not an easy one to answer because of the variables. The simplest plane, ready to fly, can cost from $75 to over $150.

The wide price discrepancy is due to R/C prices being like all others: you get what you pay for. There are dozens of radio equipment manufacturers and even more makers of kits and prefabricated planes. As with the purchase of a table model radio, the price depends on the features desired, the maker, and the quality of the parts used. There are kits for the radios, as well as kits for the planes, and building from a kit is obviously going to be cheaper than buying a ready-to-go radio and a highly prefabricated model.

The Pilot Olympia is an excellent training aircraft of the ARF variety. For .15 to .19 engines and three channels of control. Wing position makes this a high wing, or cabin type.

The Sterling Model's "Fledgling." A good beginner's plane, the Fledgling is of the shoulder-wing type in that the wing sits flush atop the fuselage. (Sterling Models, Inc.)

(NOTE: When you see the term "ARF" in advertisements, it is not by way of barking to get your attention. ARF stands for "almost ready to fly" and is a term applied to planes that require very little work to complete.)

While one needs to know absolutely nothing about radio in order to enjoy R/C, there are beginners who will wish to build their own radio receivers and transmitters. Unless the beginner has had previous experience in the assembly of electronic components, I strongly advise that he not have his first lesson with R/C equipment. Many of the parts, particularly transistors, must be soldered at controlled temperatures, otherwise the part is ruined, and too often the beginner has no idea which part or parts are damaged.

Those with experience in electronic assembly can save a considerable amount of money by putting together their own transmitters, receivers, and servos. (A servo is the unit which takes the signal sent to the receiver and converts it into action. One servo is required for each control function, although, as will be noted later, one servo can often serve two or more functions for the advanced modeler.)

There are several reliable radio kit makers offering sets with one to six channels of operation. The number of channels a set has determines the number of controls possible in the model. Boats and cars normally use but two controls, speed and steering, while airplanes use up to six channels for right and left, up and down, engine speed, ailerons, flaps, brakes, retractable landing gear, bomb drop, parachute release, and so on.

When first looking through the magazines, or around the local flying field, the beginner is confronted with an awesome variety of radio gear from which to choose. With today's reliability of

The economical way to get started in R/C is the two channel system illustrated here. Ideal for sailplanes and rudder-elevator only installations. Receiver and servos are all housed in one tidy package, popularly known as a "brick."

A bit more expensive than the two channel system, the three channel outfit offers control of rudder and elevator along with motor control, or spoilers on a sailplane. Main stick controls rudder and elevator, while the lever to the left (barely visible), is for motor or other fixed position control.

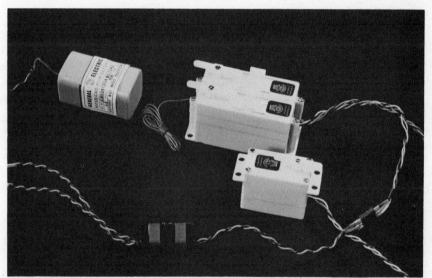

Many companies offer a conversion for the two channel systems that makes them into three channel units with the addition of an extra servo. Three channels are sufficient for most flying.

The two channel "brick," containing receiver and servos is to the right, the airborne battery pack to the left, and the switch harness in the center of this picture.

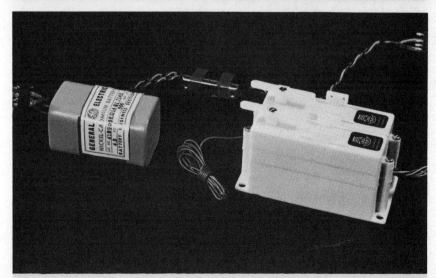

A typical four channel system. In the foreground is the receiver. Behind it is a rechargeable nickel cadmium battery pack, followed by four servos. An on-off switch is connected between the receiver and battery pack. Plug to the right of the receiver is a charge receptacle for the battery charger.

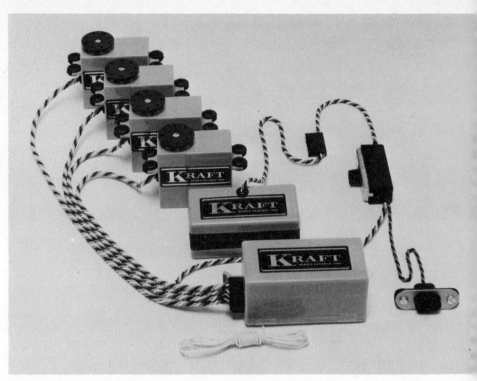

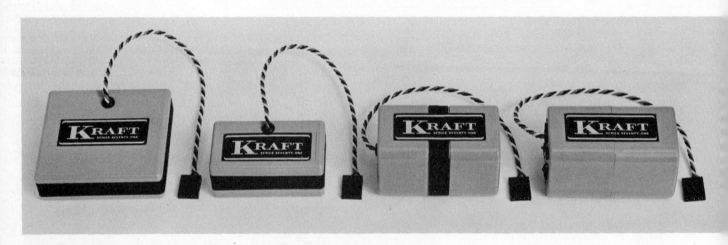

ABOVE: *Battery packs are available in several configurations from most manufacturers. From left to right: A 500 mah (milliampere hour) flat pack; 225 mah pack; 500 mah square pack; and four pencell non-rechargeable pack commonly used with most two channel "brick" systems.*

LEFT: *Almost every radio system sold today includes a charger for the rechargeable airborne and transmitter battery packs. Large plug carries current to the transmitter pack, smaller one connects to the airborne pack. Third plug (to right) plugs into standard household outlet.*

components and the keenness of competition, most radios sold are completely trustworthy. However, the wise beginner will make it a point to notice which set is most often used at a flying field, ask why, and then make his purchase accordingly. While different clubs prefer different R/C equipment, the reason is usually traced to reliability of the equipment within that club and to the most important reason of all—good service when it's needed. It must also be remembered that modelers are people, and like golfers, they want what the winner has in the way of equipment. If Joe Doaks wins the National Championships using "Frammis R/C gear," thousands of modelers will sell their reliable sets and rush to get a Frammis set, forgetting that what made Joe Doaks a winner was his flying ability, not his radio equipment.

The next things to consider in the purchase of one's first R/C set are price and level of interest. If the beginner intends to take up R/C as a mild hobby, to enjoy when time permits, or if he is of modest means, he would be wise to buy a three-channel outfit that he could use in car, boat, or plane. In car or boat he will have the previously mentioned speed and steering controls. With a plane he may have rudder, or steering control; elevator, or up and down control; and engine speed control. The beginner will use but two of the three channels on his first plane, as you will read in what follows.

For the beginner who has the money and is convinced that R/C is something he will thoroughly enjoy, most experts advise buying a set with as many channels as he can afford. However, for his first plane the beginner should *not*, under *any* circumstances, use *all* the channels. He should use but two—one for

An enlarged close-up of a digital proportional receiver showing the plug connectors. The top plug is the battery connector while the lower four are from individual servos. The antenna is the wire seen at the top of the unit.

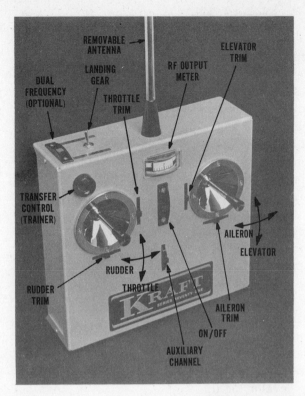
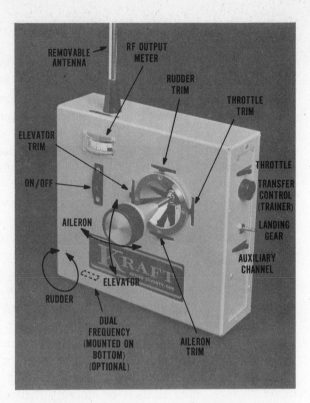

Typical six channel transmitters made by one manufacturer in two different styles. The one to the left is a two stick version, the one to the right a single stick. On the single stick model, the knob on the stick is rotated to obtain rudder control.

rudder and one for engine speed control. More channels mean more confusion, and the average beginner has his hands quite full with just two controls. While elevator control can be installed on one's first plane, it should not be used on the first flights. Engine speed will be used to climb or descend.

Another point that cannot be overemphasized is that the beginner stay away from complex airplanes, as well as from using more than two channels. Most beginners in R/C, especially modelers highly experienced in free flight or control line flying, want to start with something like a twin-engine bomber that will have all sorts of marvelous gadgets operated by their new radio equipment. FORGET IT! Even highly experienced builders have problems with scale models ("scale" means miniature copies of full-size planes), and the scale event at the yearly AMA National Championships is grimly known as the "Demolition Derby." Dozens of magnificent models are brought to this annual event by their very experienced builders, marveled at by thousands while on display, and almost a third of them are wept over by all as they crash.

Manufacturers, all modelers themselves and therefore totally absorbed in modeling, are all too often unaware of the true needs of the beginner, and instead of producing stable, slow flying and forgiving planes, they produce what is to them a "simple" plane, dub it "for beginners," and ship the kits off to the hobby shops. They are not purposely trying to dupe an unsuspecting customer; they have simply lost sight of a beginner's needs by constant exposure to R/C flying. The best type of plane, as mentioned, is a slow flying, stable, forgiving plane that will fly "hands-off." This means but one thing with *very few* exceptions; the plane should be what is known as a high-wing, or cabin, design similar to the one shown. There are a few good designs available in kit-form that have the wing mounted on top of the fuselage, or body, and this type is known as a "shoulder-wing." However, unless the beginner has a knowledgeable flyer with him at the time of purchase, he will be better off to get the high-wing type, looking for complete simplicity of structure. There should be no windows (windows normally make for weakness of structure in a beginner's plane), the fuselage should be of sheet balsa, the tail surfaces should also be sheet balsa, and the wing should be of simple but sturdy one-piece construction. The beginner will have to look at the kit plans to determine all this, and, while carefully studying the plans, he should also be sure that the wing is held on with rubber bands and that the landing gear and tail are held on with rubber bands, although this latter point is not essential.

Many manufacturers, again forgetful, are now designing planes with the wing held on by nylon bolts, the landing gear held in position with metal clips, and the tail surfaces glued firmly in place. While rubber bands holding everything together may not appeal to the purists among the beginners, when the first bad landing takes place, those rubber bands become downright lovable. Under the shock of a hard landing, or minor crash, the rubber bands snap free and allow the airplane components to come apart with little or no damage.

At a greater expense than the purchase and building of a kit, the enthusiast who wishes only to fly may purchase one of the

An excellent basic trainer for the beginner in R/C is the "Bridi R/CM Basic Trainer." A simple, straightforward design, the Bridi kit is well engineered, well thought out, and the parts are extremely well cut from top grade balsa.

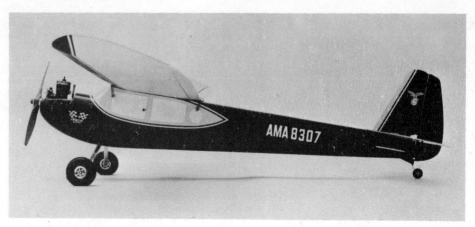

A beautiful scale model. This is where a lot of newcomers to radio control would like to begin—something to look forward to, but too much to handle in the hands of a novice flyer!

ARFs (almost ready to fly) and be airborne in the matter of few short hours. ARF planes normally have a fiberglass or high-impact plastic fuselage and wings and tail surfaces made of polyurethane, or similar foam, covered with a variety of materials. The main labor on most ARFs is the installation of engine and radio equipment.

Size of the airplane is important, and is seldom discussed in relation to the beginner. Small featherweight planes, while appearing to be the simplest of all, can often be the most frustrating. These planes have less than a 3-foot wingspan, and seldom perform properly for the novice. They normally lack stability unless a larger than specified engine is used, and this makes for a plane too fast for the average beginner to handle. If powered with the specified engine (one called for on the plans), the smaller planes tend to yaw and pitch all over the sky, and even a light breeze will add to the erratic flight behavior, leaving the beginner, back at the transmitter, at a loss as to what to try next. The experienced flyer, on the other hand, can have hours of fun with the "peanuts." One of the most famous peanuts flyers was Howard McEntee, a legend in R/C. He was the author of several works on the subject and a writer for several electronics publications. He also was former editor of *Model Airplane News*, and a past president of the Academy of Model Aeronautics, elected to their Hall of Fame in 1971 for his many outstanding achievements. He has successfully flown planes with as little as 12½-inch wingspan!

For the beginner, the best all-round size for stability, wind penetration, and ease of handling seems to be a plane with from 500 to 600 square inches wing area. Translated, this means a wing that is 56 to 60 inches long, and 10 inches wide. There is seemingly a definite relationship between the size of a model and air conditions encountered that determines performance. (Aerobatic competition flyers have all arrived at similar size planes because of this relationship.) Once over a certain size, models seem to perform more like their large-size counterparts, and, as a result, are easier to control. A great deal of this has to do with the ability to more accurately shape wing and tail surfaces on the larger models, enabling the model to more closely resemble the mathematical design characteristics of a full-size plane as determined in wind tunnels. Easy to understand if one looks at a 3-foot wing in contrast to a 6-foot wing—every mistake in building or sanding is more acute on the smaller wings, and when considering an entire airframe, the mistakes made on a smaller model tend to lap and overlap, compounding the problems.

At the other end of the spectrum is the very large size model. Not only a problem to transport, these planes, while certainly majestic and sure to draw a crowd every time they are shown, are impractical for yet another reason—there are few satisfactory power plants that will lug them surely into the air. Like the small models, they wheeze their way along, seldom accomplishing more than a bad flight that makes everyone run to hide behind the nearest parked car.

The exception to the large model rule is the glider, an excellent place for the beginner to start. Gliders are slow, they fly by themselves for the most part, and they allow the beginner precious time to get reorientated as he ends one mistake and begins yet another. In essence, learning to fly R/C is very much like learning to fly full-size planes—one starts out in the slowest and most forgiving plane possible, advancing on to the more complicated aircraft as experience and training allows. In the early days of World War II, the Luftwaffe trained most pilots of fighters and bombers by first placing them in gliders. The United States, at the same time, began flight training in the reliable and forgiving Piper Cub. While times have changed, and so have airplanes, the training methods have not. Pilots are still started off in the slowest and simplest of aircraft. This is one thing the beginner in R/C must also do. He too must begin with the slowest and simplest, otherwise his early flying days will resemble those of World War I, when there were no simple trainers or dual instruction. A pilot of that time was taken to a single-seat plane, briefly taught the controls, and then sent out to do his best. As a result, all the countries in conflict at that time lost more men in training than they did in combat. So it is with the beginners who choose to begin with planes and controls beyond their capabilities, and without the advice, and/or help of the experienced R/C'ers—they will be "shot down" forever from the ranks of happy flyers who, advancing methodically, have gone on to become "aces" at Sunday flying, or international competition.

4
Choosing a Powerplant

In Chapter Three, it was mentioned that plans specified engines of a given size. The newcomer to modeling will also usually find this information among the material printed on the kit box and perhaps wonder what the term "For engines .19 to .35" really means. It is a designation based on cubic inches of displacement, with most model engines not made in sizes much beyond 1 cubic inch of displacement. The decimal system is used to denote the precise amount of air displaced by the piston on one stroke of the cylinder. This designation also denotes the amount of power, in that the larger the displacement, the more power the engine will produce.

It is difficult to make a generalization regarding the exact size of engine a beginner should use. A great deal depends on which airplane he chooses, and how he builds it. Since most beginners tend to build on the heavy side, a rule of thumb would be that the novice, looking at a kit that calls for an engine of .19 to .35 displacement, should consider either a .23–.29 or a .35. This is a point where the aid of an experienced modeler is invaluable.

While not foolproof, the following chart offers a rough idea of engine versus airplane size:

.049—Planes up to 36-inch wingspan
.051—Planes up to 36-inch wingspan
.09—Planes up to 40-inch wingspan
.15—Planes up to 45-inch wingspan
.19—Planes up to 50-inch wingspan
.23—Planes up to 52-inch wingspan
.29—Planes up to 56-inch wingspan
.35—Planes up to 60-inch wingspan

BEST RANGE FOR BEGINNERS

.40—Planes up to 62-inch wingspan
.45—Planes up to 66-inch wingspan
.60—Planes up to 72-inch wingspan
.61—Planes up to 72-inch wingspan

If one is in doubt, it is best to use an engine on the high-power side, rather than be underpowered. As an example, let us say that the novice buys a kit for a plane that has a 56-inch wingspan. The plans say that the plane may be powered by engines from .19 to .45. Combining the chart with the information on the plans, the beginner could go one size over the chart figure and one size under the maximum recommended on the plans. This would result in a choice of an engine of .35 displacement. With almost all radio sets sold today having at least two channels, one channel will be utilized for engine control; so for the beginner's first flights, he will be using the engine speed control to keep the engine cut back for almost all the flying. In any event, it is not advisable for the beginner to get an engine larger than .35.

Which brand of engine should the beginner purchase? As with the radio equipment, the novice should ask around at a flying field about popular brands. There is quite a variation in prices of the various engines, and one will also find a variation in power for a specific displacement size from manufacturer to manufacturer. The Japanese engines are the least expensive, as might be expected, but surprisingly enough some of the Japanese engines are among the most powerful. The Italian and English engines are good performers and are among the higher priced, while the American ones are about in the middle for both price and performance, unless one orders a custom engine from one of the American manufacturers. They are almost all reliable if one treats them with the respect due these almost unbelievable little powerplants.

5
Setting Up Shop

Tools for use in R/C can be as simple or as complex as one wishes, ranging from a few basic items to a shop full of power tools. We'll begin with the basics and go on to some power equipment the serious enthusiast may wish to obtain later.

Two of the most used items in any hobbyist's possession are razor blades and straight pins. Some may wish to purchase the "razor knife" also, in preference to single-edge razor blades, so we'll discuss both. The most important feature of any knife or blade is *sharpness,* so some builders prefer the industrial razor blades available in most hardware and paint stores for about $2 a hundred. These blades are the single-edge type, have some flaw that the human eye cannot spot, and instead of ending up in a pretty package at a higher price for use on whiskers, they are packed 100 to a cheap pasteboard box to be used for paint scraping and other mundane purposes. At 2¢ a blade, a builder feels little pain in throwing one away to use a new one.

The razor knives use blades costing roughly 10¢ each, and come in a variety of styles. Some builders prefer knives because most have a pointed blade that allows one to make small precise round cuts that a razor blade couldn't handle. While hobby shops, dime stores, and the like all sell these knives in one form or another, the builder who wants the absolute ultimate in sharpness and quality goes to either a drugstore or hospital supply outfit and buys a scalpel.

Dressmaker's straight pins are used to pin parts to a plan while

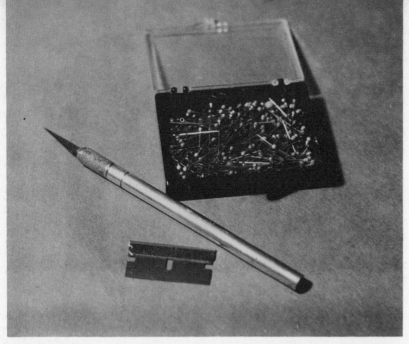

LEFT, ABOVE: *The most basic tools for the R/C hobbyist are quite simple: a box of glass bead head pins, a razor knife, and a razor blade.*

LEFT, BELOW: *Use of pins for construction. Leading and trailing edge sheeting in place. The pins in this photo are "T" pins and not the most ideal type to use because they leave large holes in the balsa. Covering will hide the holes, but the builder who wishes to go on to scale models will find that the glass-head dressmaker's pins are a neater tool to use for this purpose. The black object to the upper right is a weight used to hold the wing panel flat on plans during this stage.*

Razor Plane. So called because it uses a double-edge razor blade for its cutting blade. The left end is the front of the plane; the user's forefinger fits into the handle.

the glue is drying, and the most popular types are the ones having glass "bead" heads. These pins are very thin and therefore leave small, almost invisible holes in the wood, and the bead-like head is easier on the fingers than the small flat head of an ordinary straight pin. The beaded-head types are also easier to twist loose should glue get on them while holding two parts together.

A tool made almost solely for the modeler is an item called a "razor-plane." This is one of the handiest gadgets ever made and is used almost as much as sandpaper in shaping various balsa components. It may also be used on spruce with care, but since its cutting blade is nothing more than a double-edge razor blade, the harder the wood, the more often one must insert a new blade. Shaping leading edges of wings and other long surfaces is almost impossible to do quickly and surely without the aid of a razor-plane, and while there are various small planes and draw knives sold, there is but one true razor plane to this writer's knowledge and that is the Wil-Kro, available through some hobby shops, or from the manufacturer, Craft Master Tool Co., 23440 Lakeland Blvd., Cleveland, Ohio; price $1.50.

While the beginner may have a power drill in his tool collection, it is advisable to invest in a hand drill of reasonably good quality. There are occasions when a power drill is handy, but most drilling done in the balsa, spruce, plywood, and plastic parts requires the care and slowness of operation that only a hand drill can offer. Most often needed drill bit sizes for the modeler are $\frac{1}{16}$, $\frac{3}{32}$, $\frac{1}{8}$, $\frac{5}{32}$, $\frac{3}{16}$ and $\frac{1}{4}$ inch. Other sizes are occasionally required, but these sizes will fill most requirements.

Another tool of amazing qualities, and almost a necessity once you've tried one, is a "razor saw." It has no resemblance to a razor other than the razor thin cuts it makes through anything from balsa to brass. It is very cheap and will save a modeler many hours of frustration in dealing with various materials that require precise cutting. One of the better ones is the "Zona" saw.

The hand drill is unsurpassed for accuracy. In contrast to the electric drill, the hand type allows precision and control, as well as ease of stopping at the right time to avoid going too deeply into a surface. This is another basic tool of the R/C hobbyist.

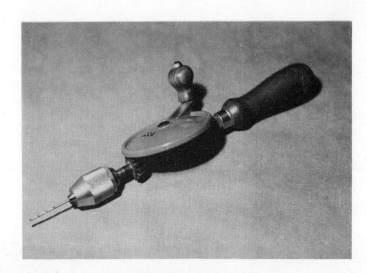

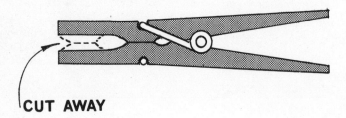

CUT AWAY

Clamp. A simple building clamp can be made from a clothespin as shown, by cutting away the two jaw "bumps." If extra grip is desired, as it may be for holding leading edge sheeting to the leading edge, cement pieces of No. 300 sandpaper inside the jaws of the clothespin.

A tool of necessity, but low in cost, is the common household clothespin. It is used in innumerable situations to hold parts, pieces, and sections while glue dries. A dozen or so of the spring type are all that's needed, and of this number about half should be modified by cutting away the two nose ends so that they are wider than they are when purchased. This is to make them have broader grip and less tension.

A simple tap and die set, available at most hardware stores, is a handy but not required item. This is used to make threads in wood or metal for various small screws or bolts of the $4/40$ or $2/56$ sizes, and also used to thread tubing or rod to fit the same-size threaded rods or bolts. Masking tape is a valuable tool for manifold usage, and while the one brand I prefer is covered in Chapter 9, you should also know that this material is used to hold many parts while glue dries. It is also used to hold plans flat on the building surface, to hold parts in place while a plane is being lined up or parts fitted, and even to wrap the package

Clothespins as a tool. Here clothespins are used as clamps while the dihedral joint is glued or epoxied in place. The object to the left is a heavy weight used to hold the left wing panel flat on building board while the other panel is blocked up to proper angle as shown on the plans. Clothespins are useful in many building situations.

in which one sends his bent radio equipment back to the manu-facturer for repairs after an untimely crash.

Small "C" clamps are also an indispensable item in the shop of a model builder. These cost about 40 cents each and their opening, between the ends of the C, are from 2 to 3 inches. These may be found in most hardware stores and many hobby shops. Like all other tools mentioned here, they will serve you for many years in both hobby and other applications.

A "gripper screwdriver" is something that few modelers can live without. This is a normal screwdriver fitted with a spring clip device that comes down over the shank of the screwdriver and grips the screw or bolt beneath its head, holding it tight into the blade of the screwdriver while the person using such a de-vice can then use one hand and place the screw or bolt into an impossible place and position it satisfactorily.

Screwdrivers of various small sizes are a necessity, as are pliers, regular and round nose, for the forming of wire parts. Wire cutters are required for wire up to $\frac{1}{16}$ inch; so when looking for regular pliers to purchase, particularly the "needle nose" type, make it a point to look for ones that also include wire cutter jaws if you're shopping on a limited budget. Otherwise, look for special wire cutters and add them to your tool collection.

For the cutting of larger wire, drilling of parts, shaping and forming of many parts, a hobbyist in R/C will eventually wish to purchase a vise. A large, heavy-duty one is to be desired, but the lighter and handier ones such as "Vacu-Vise," a vise that may be firmly clamped to any smooth work surface by simply twisting a lever, is also good. The Vacu-Vise is also good for small jobs, such as clamping parts while glue dries and the holding of parts to be soldered. The cutting of large-size "piano wire," as used for

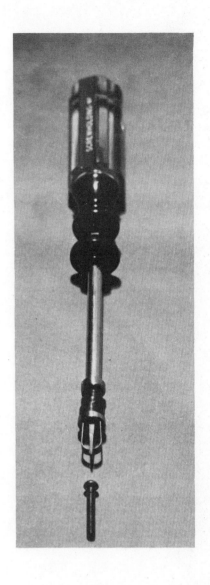

ABOVE: *Gripper Screwdriver. The small "wings" at the end of the screwdriver push down and open out to fit around the head of the bolt. Another indispensable tool for the R/C hobbyist.*

LEFT: *Using a Vise. Small-diameter wire is bent with the aid of pliers, but the large-diameter type, used for landing gears, is bent in this manner. Clamped in a vise, the wire is gently tapped with a hammer at the bend point while the other hand is used to hold the wire to keep it from whipping about. Bends are made by starting at one end and then working on through other successive angles, always keeping the long end of the wire in your hand.*

landing gears and the like, may best be accomplished by clamping the wire firmly in a Vacu-Vise or a large vise, filing notches in both sides at the cut-off point, then snapping the wire. Bending the heavy-gauge wire, such as used for landing gear, is also done with the aid of a large vise by locking the wire tightly in the vise at the bend point, then tapping the wire at the bend point with a hammer to obtain the required bend angle.

Wood rasps in small and medium sizes are good gadgets to have in one's tool collection in that they offer quick and simple means of rough-forming wood and plastic parts when the need arises. Don't get the large-toothed rasps, normally used for hardwoods, but rather the finer-toothed variety known as "mill file," both round, and semiround-flat. The round may be either ¼ or ⅜ inch for your first purchase, and these are used to slightly enlarge drilled holes in wood or metal, or to aid in the forming of wood parts calling for an inwardly curved surface. The semiround-flat mill file will be used for all sorts of wood-forming tasks.

Swiss "needle files," although not a necessity, are an inexpensive and welcome addition to any hobbyist's tool collection. These are very small files made in many shapes, and are used to solve all sorts of filing and fitting problems in both wood and metal.

A tool you should make for yourself is a sanding pad. To do this you will need a piece of *flat* board, preferably hardwood, and roughly 4 × 8 inches in surface size. Cut a sheet of medium (150 garnet or similar) sandpaper to the exact size of the wood and attach it to the wood in one of two manners: by coating the back of the sandpaper and the face of the wood with rubber cement, allowing both to dry and then bonding the paper to the wood; or by spraying both with Krylon Spray Adhesive and joining when dry. This pad is used in two ways: face up with small parts rubbed on the pad to form them, and as a sanding "block" to smooth large wood areas on the plane as construction proceeds.

A draftsman's brush is very handy to have near the building area to brush away unwanted building debris and to dust a plane before covering or doping. A "foxtail" type of brush may also be used, but it is not as satisfactory. The draftsman's brush is available at art or drafting supply stores. The foxtail brush may be purchased at hardware stores.

To this point, no tool mentioned will cost much over $3, most being in the one to two dollar range for quite good quality. Now we move to the higher priced items. . . .

A soldering "gun" is an item that is occasionally needed these days to make a solder joint in control linkages or to assemble a landing gear. Not too many years ago, a modeler couldn't go into R/C unless he had one! Still recommended for the serious modeler, these units should be of a 250-watt rating.

You will often see ads for "hand-held" power tools of seemingly endless functions. Some modelers buy them and use them constantly while others use them once or twice and abandon them as impractical. They do come in very handy with a rounded cutter blade, for uses such as hollowing out cowlings or other sections where another tool would be too large or time-consuming to use. If purchasing one, you have an option of getting one with or without all the many brushes, grinding wheels, cutters, and so on, get the one without. Most come with a catalog of available gadgetry, allowing the purchaser to select the fittings he feels he can use.

An inexpensive, lightweight vibrator type sander is ideal for use on planked sections, and at the time of this writing, Sears has one for under $10. By varying the sandpaper used, one of these lightweight units can save a lot of tedious sanding. Their action is slow enough to allow accuracy of shaping, but fast enough to be preferred over hand sanding. With almost all R/C planes and boats having planked sections of some sort, addition of one of these could be a most valued one.

One tool in my own personal shop that I find indispensable is a Dremel "Multi-Purpose, Moto-Shop." This is a small, but adequate, jigsaw-sander, and it has a power takeoff that serves all the functions of the small hand-held power tools mentioned earlier. It comes with all sorts of other gadgetry too, some useful, others not. At a lower price, and offering almost the same exact features, is the Dremel "Moto-Shop." These units are in the $30 to $60 price range and I use mine constantly for model building, as well as many other functions.

While not a true necessity, the serious modeler may wish to eventually add a drill press to his shop equipment to aid in accurate drilling, shaping, and routing. Some small units are available for use in conjunction with a power drill, but if you're interested in these miniature conversion units, avoid the so-called "bargains"; and if your power drill has any play in the chuck, abandon the idea altogether.

Although not strictly a tool in the true sense, a flush door is almost a firm requirement for use as a building board. Airframes

Wing Building-Board. Two sections of narrow flush-door are shown joined together by a piano hinge to make an adjustable, flat, building surface on which to make wings. Screws hold one side flat to the building bench, while the other side is adjustable to any degree of dihedral by moving a simple block toward, or away from, the center.

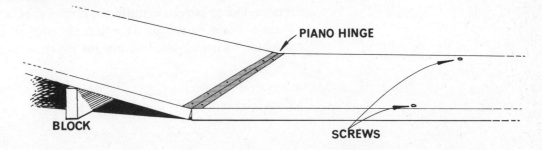

PIANO HINGE

BLOCK

SCREWS

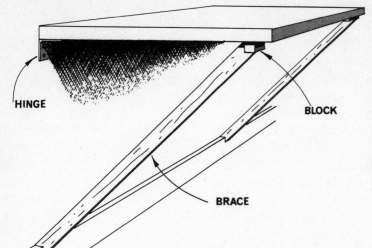

HINGE

BLOCK

BRACE

Foldaway Work-Bench. This one is made of a flush-door, held to the wall by hinges, and held upright by two "V" slotted legs that fit against baseboard and blocks glued to the underside of the door panel. When not in use, the legs are removed and the door panel is dropped to hang flush with the wall.

must be built accurately, and while many surfaces have been tried by modelers over the years, the flush door emerges as all-time winner in the flatness department, with the cheapest version, Luan mahogany, being the best due to its soft surface that allows the easy insertion of pins used to hold parts in place while the glue is drying. Many modelers buy a large flush door and use it for a workbench, placing it atop an existing frame, or hinging it to a wall and using removable legs. In my shop I have two such tables, made from flush doors, and in addition I also have a door 80 × 15 inches on which I build wings. Once the wing structure is completely pinned down, this board is stood upright in a corner, leaving the working areas clear for the next project. The door has carpeting cemented to one side (with Krylon Spray Adhesive), and this carpeted side is used for sanding and finishing steps to avoid denting the soft balsa. The carpeting traps a lot of balsa dust that would end up elsewhere and is easily vacuumed when the project is finished.

Another worthwhile idea in widespread use is the hinging of a narrow flush door in the center for use as a wing-building board. Blocking one end up allows the builder to build wings with the correct amount of dihedral in both panels. Since flush doors are hollow, once they are cut in half, wood pieces must be inserted into both halves at the cut and firmly glued in place to support the piano hinge which is recessed to lie flush with the surface. Care should be taken in fitting the insert pieces, being sure they are neither too thick nor too thin for the space in the door. Either condition will result in repeated bad wing construction.

Wing "jigs" are commercially available and are a great aid in accurate wing building. Priced in the neighborhood of $40, they are not a tool to purchase until one is sure that he will be building a good number of wings. The same is true of the fuselage jigs available. Nice gadgets, but not for everyone's needs or pocketbook.

6
Adhesives

Building a radio control plane is a good deal like building a home-made private aircraft. Many of the same materials and construction techniques are used, and many scale builders go so far as to fully duplicate full-size construction in every aspect.

Two points in building should be remembered by the beginner: one, vibration, and the damage it does to airframe, radio, and servos; and two, the stresses that R/C planes endure in maneuvers. (A meter placed in a R/C pylon racer indicated that in the turns around the pylons, the little ship was pulling a force of 30 times its own weight, or 30 Gs—more than enough to kill a human pilot!)

With vibrations and stresses firmly in mind, the beginner should, from the outset, make it a practice to build strongly but lightly, always selecting adhesives that will not be "buzzed apart" by the vibrations of the engine, or affected by flight stresses. Watching a plane come apart at the end of a loop can be quite discouraging.

Thanks to the space age, adhesives for the R/C builder, among other items, are a far cry from what they were a few short years ago. There are many adhesives available, of course, but rather than leave the beginner to grope his way through, I offer the following list of adhesives that I have found to be excellent. Please note that each has a different use in the construction of a plane.

CEMENT (fast-drying, clear; smell akin to that of nail polish). Duco—manufactured by DuPont—is sold in almost all dime

A 1915 Nieuport 11, "Bebe" parked just outside the final assembly hangar? No, it's Lou Proctor's miniature R/C version of an ultimate scale model—one any beginner can build, but should stay away from. This kind of model is what a beginner looks forward to, but never starts with—if he has any hopes of succeeding in the R/C hobby.

stores, stationers, drugstores, and groceries at 39¢ for a 1¾ ounce tube. For cleanup, use acetone or dope thinner.

I use cement in all building that is away from the immediate fuel areas, in other words: wing, tail, and fuselage behind the wing area. Balsa or spruce parts are smeared with the cement at the point of join, let dry (a matter of seconds), then recoated and joined. More than most other cements, Duco is a "penetrator" that sinks into the wood and makes for a more permanent bond. As mentioned, it is not used in areas where fuel can get to it, so if you are unsure of your abilities to cover a plane and seal it properly with a fuelproof finish (see Chapter 10, "Covering"), you had better play it safe and use one of the fuelproof types of cement such as "Sig-ment," Testors, or others, all available in hobby shops. The fuel burned in the engines is a very close cousin to paint remover, and if it works its way into a joint, as it has a habit of doing in poorly covered planes, the results are disastrous if it meets up with a non-fuelproof adhesive.

One other word of caution about *any* of the cements. Do not try to cement two surfaces or items together that have more than 2 square inches of surface area to be joined. The cements are air driers, and once shut off from the air, they will remain wet for days, even weeks.

WHITE GLUE (odorless, slow-drying, deep-penetrating, and completely fuelproof). For cleanup, use water before it dries.

FRANKLIN TITEBOND. Manufactured by the Franklin Glue Co., Columbus, Ohio, it is packaged in various sizes, the larger sizes being more economical. Sixteen ounces cost $2.45 and will build many airplanes. It is available in hobby shops, craft shops, and hardware stores.

ELMER'S GLUE-ALL. Manufactured by the Borden Co., it is packaged in various sizes, priced about the same as Titebond. The product is available in dime stores, groceries, stationers, drugstores, and the like.

These two glues are the most popular; Titebond is, in my opinion, more widely accepted by modelers as the superior product. Both are totally fuelproof and may be used to construct an entire plane, as well as the areas subject to fuel seepage. For the methodical builder they are ideal, but for the fellow who wishes speedy results, he should be warned that while these white glues appear to be dry in an hour or so, they actually require 24 hours to reach full bonding powers. Of the two, Titebond affords a worry-free grip in a shorter period, and while both may be used to secure large surface areas together, Titebond tends to set faster and grip more securely than Elmer's in such usage. In this instance, all being relative, "faster" means that you still have plenty of time to align things before the glue begins to set, normally a matter of 10 to 15 minutes, depending on the humidity in your work area. After this, Titebond tends to set faster than Elmer's.

Places to avoid the use of ANY white glue when working with balsa are places that will have to be sanded as the construction moves along. The novice will be hard pressed to plan this far ahead, so the best rule is to think along the lines of, "glue inside, cement outside." An example of this would be the construction of a wing. Placing the ribs on the spars, the modeler would observe if the joint between rib and spar was to be next to the final covering, or if the joint was to be covered by perhaps a sheet of balsa which would receive the final covering. If the former were the case, he would use the more easily sandable *cement*. If the joint was to be "inside" and therefore covered by balsa sheeting, he would use white glue. White glue, when dry, is much harder than balsa and therefore tends to resist sandpaper, while the balsa around it is quickly sanded away. Cement, on the other hand, sands down at approximately the same rate as balsa.

EPOXY (slight odor; in all cases, a *two*-part mixture, and as of this writing, anything else is not epoxy!). For cleanup, use acetone before it dries. Once dry, or set, virtually NOTHING removes it!

HOBBYPOXY. Manufactured by the Pettit Paint Co., Belleville, N.J., the product is available in various "setting time" formulas. Three-hour formula is $3 for two tubes totaling 8 ounces. One-hour formula, two tubes totaling 1½ ounces, is $1, and their "Quick-Fix," which cures in 15 minutes, is available at $2 for two tubes totaling 2 ounces. Hobbypoxy is available in hobby shops only.

"Five-Minute" Epoxy would have to hold a slight edge with any modeler due to the ultra-fast setting time, but this quickness can also be a slight drawback in some instances where the modeler wishes a bit more time to think and get things more properly aligned. This becomes a point of individual choice.

In any event, epoxy is the present day ultimate in strength, and in many instances the R/C enthusiast would be lost without it. There are few materials to which it will not adhere, and its strength is now legendary. Once a modeler has it in his shop, the uses do not stop with planes. It soon becomes a "cure-all" for everything in the house. I've personally used it to repair the rotor on the distributor of a high-priced foreign car for which parts are almost unobtainable, furniture that no glue would fix, teapots with broken handles, and every conceivable type of break on model planes. It will not bond nylon to nylon, or polypropylene articles to anything, but those are the very few materials that escape the clutches of this miracle adhesive.

Epoxy is strongly recommended for use around the fuel and

nose sections of a plane, as well as areas where high stress is likely to occur, such as wing center section joints, wing hold-down dowels or shear pin locations, and the area around landing gear support members. It is invaluable as a "smear coating" for the fuel tank compartment, adding immeasurable strength as well as total fuelproofing to this susceptible area.

Two points to remember about epoxy of any kind: First, it MUST be mixed accurately! The best manner of achieving an accurate mix is to squeeze from the rear of the tube, and to squeeze the two "beads" of mix onto ruled note paper, using the lines as a measurement guide. (I use cheap legal pads, one pad being the mixing ground for a year's modeling.) Second, epoxies can cause some strange skin irritations if one is careless in handling them. If you use epoxy and get it on your skin, do one of two things immediately—wash it off with acetone, or with soap and water. Acetone is the only thing that will truly remove epoxy in its "wet" stage, the time before it sets, but soap and water will dampen the allergenic properties of the material.

Another point worth remembering is that acetone will remove epoxy from areas where it is not wanted, but *only* if used before the "set" takes place. After that, forget it!

CONTACT CEMENT (relatively fast-drying; has an odor somewhat between alcohol and ether). Cleanup is with alcohol.

PLIOBOND. Manufactured by the Goodyear Rubber Co., it is sold in dime stores, hardware stores, and hobby shops. Approximately $1 for a 3-ounce brush applicator bottle. Cleanup is with alcohol.

KRYLON PRESSURE-SENSITIVE SPRAY ADHESIVE. Manufactured by the Borden Co., it is sold mainly in art stores, but some hobby shops have it. Price is $1.95 for a 13-ounce spray can.

Contact cements are just about what their name implies—cements that are applied to a surface, or surfaces, and then joined on contact after the bonding agent has dried. The grip, instant and never forgiving, is also, in most cases, one that never lets go. Modelers use contact cements for areas of large surface bonding, as well as smaller contact points where ultimate strength is unimportant, such as the bonding of sheet balsa to wing leading edges, balsa planking to fuselages, and so on. This is not to imply that the grip is faulty, but contact cement is seldom used for the main construction of a wooden airframe because it does not have the preferred adhesion of white glue, cement, or epoxy.

PLASTIC RUBBER (drying speed varies from brand to brand; has ammonia-like odor). Cleanup is with gasoline or naphtha.

"MAGIC RUBBER." Duro brand is manufactured by the Woodhill Chemical Corp., Cleveland, Ohio. Sold in dime stores and hardware stores, it costs about $1 for 3 ounces.

Neither the following products nor their many cousins are really true adhesives as related to building R/C planes, and yet they are indeed adhesives that prove quite valuable if used in the right places, as indicated below.

MAGIC RUBBER. If used in and around fuel compartments it affords an extra measure of closing off this area from seepage of the volatile and harmful fuel. Magic Rubber is also excellent for holding nuts for a bolt in hard-to-reach places (although epoxy should be the first consideration here), mending punctured airwheels, and the like. It is a latex rubber formula, and it dries to a semihard state.

SILASTIC. Manufactured by Dow-Corning, Corning, New York, it is sold in hobby shops, hardware stores, and craft shops—$1 for ⅞ ounce. A "bouncier" material in its dry state, it is therefore good for use in dampening vibration in an airframe by applying it around the area where a receiver is mounted to wood or where one wishes to seal an area from fuel seepage. It is also good for usage in adhering the foam rubber stripping used around wing mounts.

Some modelers use either of these two above materials to anchor their push rod installations, with Magic Rubber being the favorite after epoxy. For rubber and related materials, these two products have a definite place in the shop of the modeler who wishes to achieve positive bonding with little fuss.

CELASTIC (note the spelling!). Not to be confused with *Silastic*, Celastic is a distributed product of Sig, Montezuma, Iowa. It is sold only in hobby shops, or by order direct from Sig at a cost of 95¢ for a lightweight sheet (1/32 inch thick) of the material 9 × 18 inches. Cost for a heavyweight sheet (1/16 inch thick), 9 × 18 inches, is $1.15.

Not a true adhesive, this is an adhesive that many modelers find very valuable in creating a strong section in places where space is critical. Looking and feeling a bit like felt, Celastic is soaked in acetone or dope thinner, then smoothed into position at the desired location. When dry, Celastic is rock hard, very thin, and extremely strong. It is an ideal material with which to line fuel compartments and strengthen wing joints in that it can be cut to any shape and molded to conform to irregular curves. Its adhesion to wood is excellent.

FIBERGLASS. Available from many manufacturers and distributors, it comes as a two-part solution, plus fiberglass cloth. Solutions average about $3 for a quart; cloth is approximately $1.50 a yard. The product is available in hobby shops, boat and auto parts shops, some hardware stores. Cleanup of brushes and spills is with acetone while "wet." Nothing removes fiberglass once it has "cured."

Fiberglass is used quite extensively by some modelers, and the ones who've taken the time to learn the methods involved in its usage have turned out some superb models. Using the material to construct fuselages, wheel pants, cowlings, and the like, the serious modeler arrives at a very strong, lightweight, and highly durable structure, as well as a very finely finished one.

To construct a fuselage, as an example, the modeler first carves the fuselage from balsa or pine, sanding and finishing this form to absolute perfection. He then coats the unit with a parting agent, such as silicone spray, then proceeds to lay strips of the fiberglass cloth over the form, coating each with the mixed two-part solution, called "resin." The strips of cloth are built up until there is approximately $\frac{1}{16}$- to $\frac{3}{32}$-inch thickness to the laminations. This makes the "female" mold, which is then cut lengthwise top and bottom and removed from the original wooden form. The process is reversed, placing parting agent in the female mold, then laying strips of cloth and the mixed resin into it to a depth of roughly $\frac{1}{16}$ inch. In this manner, one can build quite a number of fuselages from the one mold.

The mixing of the two solutions to make the resin is somewhat different from the mixing of the two ingredients used in epoxy. While epoxy mixture must be quite exacting, mixing of fiberglass resin depends on the whim of the modeler. The more of the hardening agent used, the faster the curing time, and if too much is used, one can hardly finish stirring before the resin turns very hot, and the mix is solid. Normally, the directions given on the can are too slow for modeling use, unless one purchases the product as repackaged for the modeler. Most, packaged for the boat builder, call for rather cool mixes that allow a boat builder time to work the material over large surfaces. A little experimentation can quickly show how many drops of hardener to add to get the curing time desired. Only small amounts are mixed at a time, using cheap paper cups as containers. Brushes used should also be cheap and dispensable.

Another use for the resin, and often the cloth, is the fuel-proofing of engine and fuel areas, such as the forward part of the fuselage, wing dihedral joints, and the underside forward portions of fuselages on gliders. (Once onto the magic properties of fiberglass and epoxy, the modeler will find dozens of new ways to fix old bugaboos around the house. Fiberglass on lawn furniture ends, once and for all, the problem of rot or rust!)

RUBBER CEMENT. Available from art supply stores, dime stores, drugstores, and so on, it sells at varying prices and in varying amounts. Milky whitish, it comes in thicknesses that vary with the place purchased—art supply houses carrying the purer, uncut type. It can be thinned with rubber cement thinner only. Cleanup is by rubbing away the dried cement.

Rubber cement can be used in two ways: first, by brushing on a coat and immediately placing the item to be held on the wet cement; second, by coating both surfaces, allowing them to dry, and then putting them together. Neither is permanent, but the latter affords the better bonding method. Modelers use rubber cement in places where little stress or strain will occur, and they use it in the final paint trimming of a plane by cutting their designs and numbers from onion skin tissue and with one coat cementing the tissue onto the plane. Once the cement dries (a matter of minutes), the excess cement is rubbed away with the fingers, and paint is sprayed onto the tissue's open areas. Called a "frisket," the tissue is easily pulled off when the paint is dry, and the remaining cement rubbed off. Using the double coating method with drying, then bonding, rubber cement is used to affix striping on windshields, instruments in detailed cockpits, and similar decoration.

7
Solvents and Cleaners

In this age of "Miracle Products," solvents and cleaners appear on the market almost daily, making it virtually impossible to offer any sort of advice on their usage. However, there are some basic old standbys that will take care of almost all of a modeler's needs. These are:

ACETONE. Colorless, extremely flammable, it has a strong smell of the type associated with fingernail polish. Cost varies around the United States, but an average would be about $2 a gallon. Acetone is sold in paint and hardware stores, with drugstores selling the ultrapure kind at a *greatly* higher price.

For those aware of its uses, acetone is somewhat of a cure-all in the field of solvents and cleaners. It is an excellent thinner for butyrate dope (butyrate dope is also referred to as "hot fuelproof" or "fuelproof"). Acetone is used to remove unwanted epoxy and fiberglass resin before they set; to clean metals prior to soldering; to clean off soldering flux after soldering; to remove unwanted model cement, wet or dry; to remove dope, enamel, varnish, and the like from paint brushes; and as a cleanup agent for many of the space age adhesives.

It also has some drawbacks: Spilled on floors or painted surfaces, it will eat its way into almost all encountered, destroying the finish. *Containing ketone, it can cause heart and brain hemorrhaging in those who are foolish enough to use it for prolonged periods without adequate ventilation.*

ALCOHOL. Colorless, flammable, the cheapest type of rubbing alcohol is perfectly adequate and may be purchased in drugstores and groceries. This type averages about 30¢ a pint.

Use alcohol to clean all plastics, such as windshields and canopies; to clean fuel from a plane after flying; to clean dirty engines, and as a cleanup agent for many adhesives. It will *not* remove cement, epoxy, fiberglass resin, or white glue, but *will* work on many of the rubber-base products.

LIGHTER FLUID. It is also colorless, flammable. As with alcohol, look for the cheapest brand available in supermarkets or drugstores. Average cost is around 30¢ a pint.

The use of lighter fluid somewhat parallels that of alcohol, in that it is an excellent cleaner to use in removing fuel from a plane, good for use on many plastics, and since it comes in metal cans it is handy to take along in a field box for cleanup jobs. (Lighter fluid and alcohol are also good to remove those nasty little price stickers that stores put on products, as well as the indelible ink prices applied with a rubber stamp.)

"408," FANTASTIK. Many modelers carry a spray bottle of one of these two products along in their field boxes for plane cleanups. They work fast and efficiently, but in the author's experience, they can leave a residue, so the fussy modeler will want to do further cleanup when arriving home after a day's flying. While the careful modeler will clean his engine with alcohol after each flying session, residue gum does build up. Occasional use of one of these products and a good stiff toothbrush will remove it, unless left too long (see also next paragraph).

FRY PAN CLEANER. Sold by various makers of electric frying pans, all are about the same in makeup and cleaning ability. Since the cleaner is designed to cut away fats and greases baked onto aluminum and steel pans at temperatures ranging up to 475 degrees, the cleaner is ideal for cutting away baked-on oil residues from engines. Model engines run at the same temperature, 475–6 degrees, and the cleaner makes easy work of making an engine look new again as well as bringing back efficiency. When using it, plug the intake venturi and exhaust with pieces of dust-free rags so the cleaner cannot get inside the engine.

LIQUID DETERGENT. Take your choice. Any of the types used for dishwashing are fine as cleaners for planes after flying, and for use in cleaning fiberglass and other plastic parts to remove mold release residue before assembly. Mixture with water is not critical.

"WET TOWELS." Perhaps a funny thing to include, but the chemical wet-pack paper towels are a most welcome addition to a flyer's field box for the quick removal of fuel residue from one's hands. Available in drug and grocery stores at various prices for various size packages.

BORAX. The 20-mule-team effort of this product in modeling is unknown to many. Borax is a "super-sucker," and for models where fuel has seeped into woodwork, a good layer of Borax will lift it out overnight. Only use when the engine has first been removed.

8
Kits

While, like most beginners, you are anxious to get your new kit assembled into something flyable, do take time to study the plans, as well as all the pieces, before beginning the pinning and glueing. These "Search and Enjoy Missions" can save a lot of frustration as the building progresses.

Start with the plans and read them thoroughly. Rolled plans can be straightened by rolling them in the opposite direction, and folded plans can best be put into usable condition by ironing them as one would a sheet. In any event, *flatness* is important; folds and wrinkles can cause unwanted flaws in building since all of the airframe is normally pinned down on the plans during the building process.

With the plans flattened and read, you should start sorting out the parts. In most kits the parts are die-cut but often remain a part of the balsa sheet in which the cuts were made. If these parts do not push out easily, put the cut side face down and sand the back side with fine or medium sandpaper attached to a sanding block. This sanding should go quite quickly, allowing the parts to drop out of the sheet freely. If you see that the parts are holding and that a good amount of balsa must be sanded away in order to free them, stop the sanding and use a razor knife to cut them free. (If the parts are cut into a $\frac{1}{8}$-inch-thick sheet, and you have to wear off $\frac{1}{32}$ to $\frac{1}{16}$ inch to get them loose, the parts will be too thin to fit properly into the frame.)

If any of the wood in the kit, sheets, strips, and so on, is pulpy, the best practice is to replace it with good firm stock. Do likewise with wood that is rough cut, since sanding out the roughness usually takes away too much thickness for the wood to be of any value. The inclusion of such woods in a kit is not too frequent, but it does happen, and to use them is to ask for structural failure or a lot of extra work for poor results.

Before throwing out any defective parts, use them as a template to cut new parts from better wood. In the event that a part is completely defective to the point of being unusable as even a template, don't panic. Most plans show each part in outline, and you may cut a new one from this outline drawing. The simplest means of doing this accurately is to turn the plan over, place it against the window, blacken the area behind the desired part with a soft lead pencil (No. 1 or 2), and then, using a cotton ball or a wadded facial tissue soaked in alcohol or lighter fluid, rub the pencil-blackened area lightly. This turns the pencil rubbings into a solid black film of high-grade carbon. Carbon paper can be used of course, but the results, due to thickness and possible slippage, are not as satisfactory as the method outlined. You might also make note of this method for the many times you will need it in future building, and also remember that if you ever encounter a dark surface where pencil carbon will not show, simply use white, yellow, or orange chalk on the back side of the drawing to be transferred, *but,* instead of using lighter fluid or rubbing alcohol, use the cotton ball or facial tissue *dry,* with just enough pressure to spread the chalk evenly.

As you separate the parts from the die-cut sheets, match them with the plans to determine where they belong. Then put each into a separate pile, one pile for the fuselage, one for the wing, one for the rudder, and so forth. A good practice here is to use small labeled box lids, such as those from shoeboxes, with each lid holding the parts for a specific phase of construction. As you build, you can simply reach for the box labeled "Wing" and not worry about sifting through all the other parts to find the ones needed to build the wing.

Should any of the die-cut parts split as you push them clear of their sheet, cement them back together at once rather than risk losing or damaging the pieces. Too, some parts can break on such a clean line that they, if not cemented back together at once, will later look like completely different parts. Note that I've used the word "cement" and not "glue." This is important in that the part may be one that will be exposed on the finished airframe, and if you will remember the section on adhesives, you will remember that glue, when dry, is mean stuff to sand; so play it safe and use cement on any broken pieces.

If there are small bags with nuts and bolts, or other small parts, best bet is to leave them bagged until needed, marking the bags as to where they go, and then putting these too in the proper box lids. Small parts often get lost when removed from their original package and left to roll around in a kit.

Almost no kit produced in America contains all that is required to make a finished airplane. Cements and glues are left out to avoid fires in transit, or while items are stored, and, too, there is always the possibility of the adhesive's container becoming punctured and sticking the whole works together. Wheels are omitted for several reasons, the main one being the extra cost it would add to the selling price of the kit. There is also the matter of deterioration if wheels are left to sit in a kit in some climates, plus the fact that model builders develop favorites among wheels and other parts and wouldn't use the ones supplied anyway. The same holds true for all the control linkages and the covering material, although some kit makers do include these latter two items.

If covering is included with the kit, make it one of the first items to be taken out of the kit and stored away in a safe place. If you intend to use it, you will want it clean and unwrinkled when it comes time for the covering job.

If the kit should have foam wings, these too should be treated with great care until you are ready to cover them. Styrofoam, once covered, makes a very strong and relatively damage-free wing, but since styrofoam is highly susceptible to denting and breakage, before covering with balsa, or one of the plastics available, put the wing panels in an out-of-the-way place where they will remain clean and safe from damage. One way to insure their protection, as well as their cleanliness (cleanliness is important because they will have to be thoroughly coated with an adhesive to accept the final "skin"), is to wrap each panel in a plastic bag such as the ones that come back on dry-cleaned clothes. And, speaking of these bags, if you find clear ones, they are excellent to tape over a plan to keep the parts from sticking to the paper during the pin-down and glueing stages.

This sorting and indexing procedure is all important in getting to know a kit and its peculiarities. *Never* try to just unroll the plans and begin building. To do so will result in total chaos. It's far better to spend an evening or two in leisurely study of all the parts and pieces as related to the plans.

9
Construction

Many adults, after building models in their younger years, return to the hobby when they see their first R/C plane. Many of the building techniques remain the same, but there are many new ones that came about from the advent of the readily available space age "wonder" materials. In this chapter we'll review the old techniques and get into some of the new ones, hopefully passing along a few tricks that may prove helpful to both the newcomer and the reenlisted.

As mentioned earlier, the framework is pinned to a building board with straight pins at almost all beginning stages of construction in order to assure trueness of structure and ease of building. Pins are also used at many other construction stages and often wrongly in that they do not do the proper holding job.

Masking tape and rubber bands are invaluable "tools" and should be a part of every modeler's workshop. Masking tape is particularly useful for jobs like the joining of two sheets of balsa, edge to edge. With the sheets on a flat surface and abutting each other, tape is run full length over the intended joint. One applies glue or cement (cement is best if the joint is to be sanded later) between the sheets by bending the sheets back on their recently applied tape. Then, with the taped and cemented sheets lying down on a flat surface, tape is also applied to the joint on the reverse side. The unit is then set aside to dry and may, in fact, be stood upright in an out-of-the-way place. The tape keeps the wood flat and holds the two sections together, and when the tape is removed later, the joint is almost invisible.

A word of caution about masking tape: I've tried almost a dozen different brands of tape, and while most of it was good to seal wrapped packages, most of it was lousy for use in model building. I've found but one tape trustworthy enough for the many uses a modeler has for it and this is 3M brand "Scotch" masking tape. It doesn't separate, the adhesive is well balanced for all-around use, and it has enough elasticity to bend and fit for most applications. When you are painting a model, the true qualities of masking tape become very evident. Some tapes do not seal off the masked area at all, but rather allow the paint to seep under its edges. Others have so much grip that, when removed, they pull off the paint beneath. While the 3M is a bit more expensive than most others, it's much cheaper in the long run and a lot less frustrating to use.

The word "accurate," as applied to the airframe, appears many times in this book, and simply cannot be overstressed. Built-in warps cannot be removed like ones incurred due to atmospheric changes, and they can wreak havoc, especially on a novice's plane where he has his hands full learning the normal flight routine, let alone fighting the effect of airframe warps.

If you've never built a model, or you've been away from them for a long period, do yourself a favor and obtain an all-balsa, rubber-powered model with about an 18-inch wingspan, and find yourself a field on a windless morning or evening. When assembling the model, carefully look at the flying surfaces to see if there are any warps. Leave them alone if they exist and make a flight to observe what the warps do to the flight characteristics. Remove the warps (hold the surface to be corrected close to your mouth, and gently breathe hot moist air on it while you twist in the opposite direction of the warp), then try another flight to see what happens.

Change the torque setup by twisting the propeller bearing to the right, then later to the left. This will quickly demonstrate the effect of engine alignment on a plane's performance. The rubber model will have a natural turning tendency due to the torque of the spinning propeller, and is desirable in a free-flight model where the object is to gain as much altitude as possible as quickly as possible. In a radio-controlled plane, *straight* flight is desired, with the pilot making any turns from the transmitter. Therefore, most plans will indicate a specific amount of "right thrust" as well as a specific amount of "down thrust." Inaccuracy in building can change these settings, and what may seem to be a bit of misalignment in structure to the inexperienced builder can cause serious flight problems, as demonstrated by the adjustments made to the rubber-powered model. The engines used in R/C planes have tremendous torque, and the variance of even 1 degree right or left, up or down, can make an otherwise good airplane fly poorly.

Fuselage and tail group are laid out showing the primary components.

Don't let all this information terrify you. Just be well aware that accuracy is important and build with this in mind at all times. A few small devices can aid greatly in obtaining accuracy, and one of them is a small steel square, such as used by carpenters. This device is handy for use as a cutting guide for small straight cuts, as well as in its more important function of aiding the modeler in obtaining absolutely square joints where called for (such as around the firewall section of many planes), in the placement of the wing ribs in a true vertical position, and in alignment of tail surfaces.

Modelers fall into habits. Some always build the fuselage, or body of the airplane first, while others prefer to build the wings and get them out of way, then go on to the relatively easier fuselage and tail assemblies. My habit is to begin with the fuselage, so I'll begin with it here too.

Whether slab-sided (side cut from one sheet of balsa) or of built-up construction (constructed from sheet and strips), every fuselage has two sides: a right and a left. Although normally identical, each side has an inside and an outside, and this should be kept in mind as you begin working.

The easier method of obtaining accuracy (that word again!) is to build both sides at the same time. In the case of slab-sided construction, where the entire side is precut, place one of the sides

on the side view of the fuselage and carefully position it for alignment with the lines indicating front and rear of the body. Next,
slide the side up enough to be able to see former positions at the
bottom of the fuselage plan. Recheck the ends for alignment; then
pin the side to the plan in this position and, using a ballpoint pen,
accurately mark former positions with a ruler. A method I use
with great success is to initially mark the *plan* with a ballpoint
pen, continuing all former and bulkhead lines beyond the outline
of the fuselage. Then, pinning the side into exact alignment with
the drawing, I merely use the drawn extension lines as a guide
to mark the balsa sides.

The next move in slab-sided construction is to pin down the
opposite side parallel to the first, with the two tops facing each
other. (Assume the top to be the straightest; otherwise face the
bottoms of the sides to each other.)

Working with the lines marked on the one side, a ruler is used
to continue the lines over onto the other piece as it lies parallel
with the marked one, thus assuring duplicate positioning of
formers or bulkheads. If stiffeners, such as square or rectangular
strips, are called for, these are glued in position at this time, with
the sides pinned flat to avoid warpage. If the plan calls instead for
formers to be placed on the lines marked, proceed to the next step.

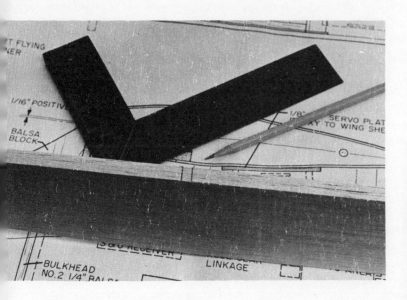

*The first step is to mark the location
of all fuselage formers on the fuselage
sides.*

*Positioning Bulkheads. Be sure to use
a carpenter's square to properly locate
their position.*

Placing formers accurately between two slab sides is done by pinning the formers to the plan in an upright position directly over the top view of the fuselage, using the triangle to assure their being at 90 degrees to the plan. Once all are pinned in place and checked to be sure that tops are up and bottoms are down, the sides are put in place, placing glue along the previously marked lines, then placing the side against the upright formers. Pins can be used to hold the side in place, but if it is curved, the best method is to use jars filled with wet sand as holding weights against the outer portion of the side piece. Also of aid here is

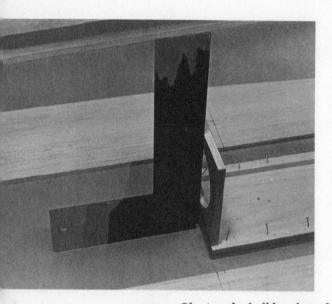

LEFT: *Glueing the bulkheads to the top sheeting and checking alignment with a carpenter's square.*
RIGHT: *Joining the top sheeting with bulkhead in place to the fuselage sides.*

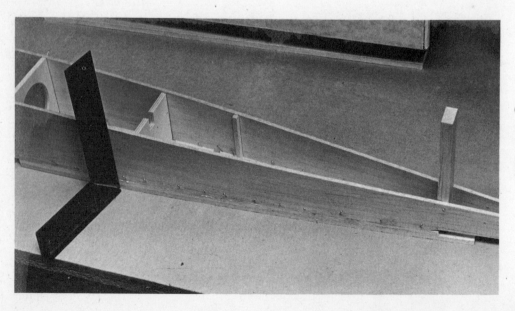

Check alignment with a carpenter's square as the fuselage bulkheads are glued in place to the sides.

Popsickle sticks are shown here as handy glueing clamps when used in combination with rubber bands. Note that the small C clamps have blocks of wood between them and the fuselage sides to avoid denting the wood and to give a long, even pressure.

Masking tape and/or rubber bands are used as shown here where it is not possible to use clamps.

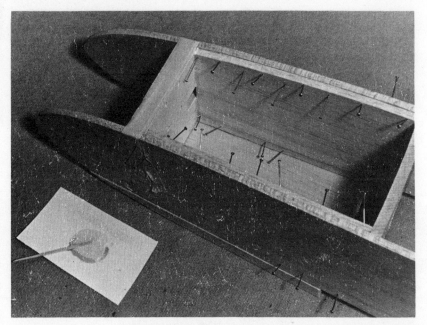

ABOVE: Firewall and fuel compartment doublers are epoxied in place.
RIGHT: The nose doublers and beam motor mount supports are epoxied in place in assembly.

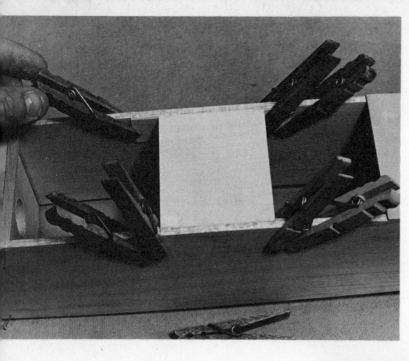

Main landing gear support braces, of ⅟₁₆-inch plywood, are epoxied and clamped in place with clothespins until dry.

Fuselage plywood sheeting for lower front is glued and taped in place until dry.

Balsa fuselage sheeting for bottom rear is glued and pinned in place following the plywood sheeting.

masking tape at the front and rear to hold the sides to the front and rear formers. Add the second side in the same manner, and allow the glue at least three to four hours to set thoroughly before doing more. Often, at this stage, one can add top or bottom sheeting, but, in so doing, should be very careful not to shift the frame in any manner and to be able to remove the frame from the board once the sheeting is in place. Pins buried beneath a solid mass of wood can be rather discouraging when one discovers he must somehow remove them.

Once the initial fuselage construction is sufficiently dry, remove it from the pinned position and add top and/or bottom pieces as called for on the plans. Be sure, when using white glue, to allow at least three hours for drying. What may appear dry is really not until this time period elapses, and even then one can encounter looseness if a part or parts are in place under tension. Safest bet is to let the frame dry overnight before removal from the board.

Before final placement of pieces that seal up the fuselage, check the plans to see what, if any, pieces need to be put in position while you can still reach in to do so. This would include push rods, engine bearers, servo rails, landing gear plate, and so on.

A built-up fuselage, or one constructed of mainly strip wood,

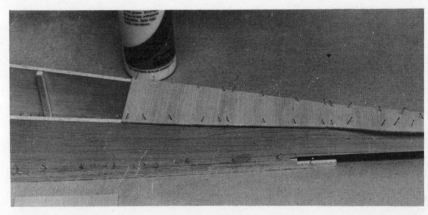

ABOVE: *Top rear sheeting is glued and pinned in place using Titebond glue.*
BELOW: *Top rear sheeting—a close-up view.*

LEFT, ABOVE: *Beam motor mounts might have to be trimmed to fit your particular engine mount spacing.*
LEFT, BELOW: *Trimmed Motor Bearers fit the chosen engine— in this case a Veco .61.*
BOTTOM: *Thrust angles are checked while engine is temporarily positioned.*

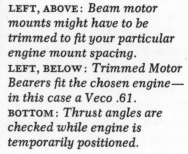

is built by making both sides at the same time, pinning parts for both directly on top of each other. Squares of wax paper are placed between the pieces wherever glue is to be applied so that the two sides are not permanently joined together when the glue dries.

When cutting uprights and longerons, cut two at a time so they are identical in length, and put them in place before cutting the next pair. This will insure an exactly matching pair of sides. Top and bottom spreader pieces are cut the same way, two at a time, and here the top ones (or bottom if the bottom of the side pieces should be straight) are pinned in position on the plans and the two side pieces are pinned against them after glue has been applied at the proper points. The matching set of spreaders is then added to the bottom (or top), taking care to place them exactly to coincide with their mates across the way.

Further fuselage construction will vary from model to model, but as long as one gets the basic frame straight and true, the further additions will go relatively easy. One point to check before things get too far along is the complete fuelproofing of the forward, or nose, sections of the fuselage. Being sure that all the required structure is in place and that slightly oversize holes are drilled for throttle linkages, steerable nose wheel push rod, and so on, the builder then mixes a batch of fuelproofing and applies it liberally to the tank compartment, the firewall (front and rear), and any exposed wood that may come in contact with fuel. (I normally leave this operation until such time as the nose is completely sanded to shape, and I also coat the outside of the nose for a distance back to the leading edge of the wing on the exterior, as well as the interior.)

There are several solutions one may use for this fuelproofing but the leading favorite is fiberglass resin, with two coats applied

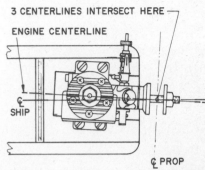

RIGHT THRUST SHOWN - ANGLE BETWEEN SHIP C.L. & ENGINE C.L. IS THRUST ANGLE

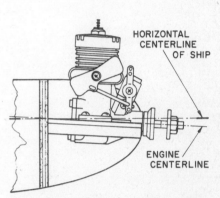

DOWN THRUST - ANGLE BETWEEN HORIZONTAL C.L. & ENGINE C.L. IS THRUST ANGLE

Fuelproofing the inside of the engine compartment and all adjacent areas is best accomplished with polyester resin.

to make sure the wood is thoroughly sealed, including those previously mentioned holes where linkages and push rods will go through bulkheads and firewall. Glow engine fuel is one of the worst penetrators and destroyers known, and, give it a crevice to seep into, it will dissolve a whole framework!

Another smart move to make when applying the fiberglass resin is that of also adding a layer or two of fiberglass cloth to further strengthen the nose area on the outside. The finer grade of cloth is used for this purpose, with the resin painted about an inch or so past the end of the cloth, going toward the tail. This will allow an easier sanding of the finished fiberglass. The addition of this glass cloth will add a tremendous amount of strength to a beginner's plane that will come in for its share of hard knocks when landing—or skittering into all sorts of things on takeoffs.

Fiberglass resin has, at best, a hanging, putrid smell that offends most "civilians" and a great number of modelers, if the truth were known. If you choose to use it, plan to do so with an open window and an exhaust fan or, better yet, outside. An alternative method of fuelproofing with less odor is that of smearing a coat of epoxy glue over the previously mentioned areas. You may also utilize the strength of fiberglass cloth, using the glue in place of the standard resin, and your family will feel less hatred for your new hobby. "Hot batches" of fiberglass, or ones that cure quickly, will help a lot in reducing the time that the smell will hang on. Some say that to use the hot batch (mixing a larger than recommended portion of hardener with the resin) results in loss of strength, but the main purpose here is to obtain fuelproofing and not primarily to obtain strength. I have always used the hot-batch method, and I've had planes come in to skid along concrete on their noses with no real damage other than some skinned paint which was quickly retouched.

Other fuelproofings for use around the nose are the various epoxy paints and acrylic enamels. These are normally applied as a finishing process for the entire model and done after the model is completely covered; but the careful builder will wish to put several coats in the fuel areas, again being sure to coat every exposed edge. This is discussed further in the chapter dealing with finishes.

At this point, wing and tail saddles (cutouts in the fuselage where these surfaces fit) should be checked for trueness, being sure that one side is not lower or higher than the other.

With most fuselages having square sides, checking the saddles is easily done. Simply place a carpenter's tri-square or combination square on edge at right angles across the saddle and check to see if the right angle part of the square fits snugly against the fuselage sides. Make a note of whatever amount of wood must be added or removed to make the saddle square, *but do not add or cut at this time!* Modifications to the saddles are only made after the wing and elevator are finished and put in place, since building flaws in either of those surfaces can possibly correct the flaws in the saddles. Variations can and do happen. Balsa wood is a far cry from maple or steel, and even final sanding can bring about changes in saddle settings that are barely noticeable— until measured out at the wingtips.

Most tail surface construction is easy and quite straightforward, but since this portion of the airplane controls half the flight, care must again be taken to be sure that no warps are built into the structure. If elevator halves are joined by dowel or wire, this joiner must be firmly affixed to the two surfaces. For dowel, use white glue or epoxy. For wire, epoxy. Although not often shown on many plans, further joining power is obtained by the addition of cloth strips wrapped over the joiner at right angles and cemented to the elevator top and bottom for a distance of about an inch in from the joiner. Once buried under the final covering, this cloth reinforcement adds a great deal of strength. Silk is ideal for this use in that it is light in weight and extremely strong.

A note here about weight. An airplane is normally balanced somewhere around a point one-third of the way back from the leading edge of the wing. Keep this firmly in mind when building, and try to keep the tail components light, but as strong as possible. For every 1 ounce of extra weight in the tail, you will have to add about 3 extra ounces to the nose to achieve balance. While lead ballast is added to some planes, it is best to learn how to build in a manner that will avoid this extra cargo.

Put the tail surfaces aside with the fuselage, and clear the board for construction of the wing. Go over the plans carefully and note whether or not "washout" is called for, and if it is, add

To assure 90-degree alignment of parts, use the carpenter's square. Accuracy is important in construction and the few extra minutes spent in the use of such tools assures trouble-free airframes where flight performance is concerned.

Wing frame pinned to the building board with center section marked for cutting after wing is completed in the initial stages. Note the "webbing" pieces inserted between the ribs, with wood grain running vertically between the spars. The webbing adds tremendous strength to the wing structure. Dihedral brace is seen lying just forward of the wing frame.

Moisten leading edge sheet with a damp sponge so it will more easily form to the contour of the ribs.
Close-up view of the leading edge sheeting ready to be formed to the contour of the ribs.

RIGHT: *Glue the leading edge sheeting to the ribs and the main spar, and hold in place with masking tape and pins.*
BELOW: *Glue all cap strips in place and hold with pins until dry.*

RIGHT: *Center section sheeting is added in wing construction.*
BELOW: *Top and bottom stabilizer sheets are temporarily joined with a piece of masking tape.*

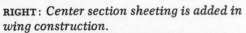

Bend the stabilizer sheets back on the masking tape and join together with a bead of Titebond glue; then weight down on a flat surface until dry.

the right-size pieces of scrap wood at the appropriate spots before doing anything else. Washout is a method of using a built-in "twist" of the wing surface to keep the tips from stalling out before the center section. Not all planes have this "twist," but if it's called for, be sure you build it in.

Next, look for an end view of a wing rib, or ribs, to determine the exact structure called for. These views will normally show the builder what pieces must be placed on the plan first. Ignoring these drawings can lead to a lot of mistakes and bad wing construction.

Wing ribs normally call for a spar on which they rest, or are fitted. Die-cutting often is inaccurate enough to make the spar slots in the ribs vary from rib to rib, and the builder who tries to pin the ribs accurately in place will have a great deal of trouble in doing so. Many will try to force the alignment and succeed beautifully—only to find unexpected warps in the finished wing. Never force parts to fit by wedging them in place; they'll only do as they wish later in the game. Best method for alignment of ribs is to pin down the leading edge, then pin the ribs in their correct place, *flat* not upright; lay a straightedge over them in line with the indicated spar position, and mark each one, at the front and rear edge of the spar lines. Do the same at the rear edge of the ribs where the plan shows that they should end. Next, take the ribs off the plan and trim them where they need it, or add scrap wood to places where the spar cutout is too large.

If all the ribs are the same size, and most are on beginners' planes, one may find a rib that most closely matches the end view shown, then use it as a master to mark and cut all the other ribs. Another method is to slide all the ribs onto a short length of spar stock, pack them together, and sand them to the same exact size, as one would sand a block. This may result in a very slight mismatch with the plans, but the important thing is to have all ribs and spar cutouts identical to obtain a "true" wing.

Almost every wing calling for a sheeted, or planked, leading and trailing edge has this sheeting or planking added while the wing is still pinned to the building board. Should the wood supplied for this purpose be very stiff ("C" grain in wood chart), replace it with A or B grain stock. Wet the top side of the sheet with hot water after the sheet has been carefully cut to fit its position, and cement or glue it in place, using pins to hold it while the adhesive dries. Some builders use contact cement to fasten the planking, but I don't recommend it for beginners unless they are familiar with the use of this product.

Fitting final sheeting between the leading and trailing edge planking often stumps beginners. It is done by working toward the center and the last piece cut and fit as follows: lay a piece of wood, wider than the gap to be filled, on top of the gap. Use pins to hold it in position, then lay a straightedge on top of the top piece and use it as a guide to cut through the top piece and the planking beneath, cutting parallel to the wing and other planking. Repeat this on the other edge of the top piece. With care in cutting, the top piece should drop in for a perfect fit after the edge scraps of the planking below are removed. This method is also used in making repairs and in splicing two pieces together.

If the model being built has a foam wing (one shaped from styrofoam or similar material) and this wing requires sheeting to be applied over it as a "skin"; the best method, unless otherwise specified on the plans, is to glue the sheeting together before placing it on the foam surfaces. This is done with masking tape strips as mentioned in the beginning of this chapter.

When both wing sections, or panels, have been completed, one section is pinned in place over its plan, then the other is joined to it, using blocks at the one wingtip to assure alignment and the proper degree of dihedral. In making this important joint, do not be stingy with glue! Where dihedral braces are called for, be sure they are well coated with glue or epoxy, and extend the adhesive an inch or so beyond the end of such a brace to form a "skin" on the spar for even more strength. If a reinforcing tape is suggested on the plans, *don't omit it!* Even if none is suggested, it's wise to add one, for this small strip of cloth adds a considerable amount of strength to the wing center. Normally, this strip is roughly an inch wide, runs the full width of the wing, overlapping itself on the opposite side, and is of fiberglass cloth or sturdy cotton tape such as used by dressmakers. The latter is available in dime stores at notions counters. This tape is put in place before covering and is usually held with cement—with the cement being spread a distance beyond its edges for further strength. This accent on the wing center section strength is due to the fact that R/C planes normally operate under far higher gravity loads ("Gs") than any full-size plane ever hopes to encounter. While the strongest of fighter planes in combat situations seldom go through a force of 10 Gs, models regularly encounter forces around 15 Gs on pull-outs.

Once the entire frame is completed, carefully sand it smooth with the aid of a sanding block, or a vibrator sander. This is the stage where you will find out if all your glue joints are good ones or bad ones. Even if all goes well and the frame remains in one piece, take time to probe and pull at the various parts to be sure the joints are solid. Surface joints are easily recemented, but interior points can often pose a problem. For these I use a length of plastic tubing (push-rod tubing is ideal) forced into the end of a tube of cement or glue bottle. This flexible extension can get into almost any nook or cranny to deliver the adhesive direct to the spot where needed. A large hypodermic needle, such as a veterinarian uses, may be used for the same purpose.

To backtrack a bit, several construction operations often stump the beginner. Here are some of the problems, and my method for solving them:

DRILLING HOLES IN THE ENGINE MOUNTS. Assuming that the model being built calls for wood motor mounts, and the mounts must be drilled to receive the four bolts that hold the engine in place, the mounts are usually drilled *before* being built into the plane. Unless using the exact engine shown on the plans, ignore the mounting holes indicated and instead use the drawing of the engine as a guide for placement of *your* powerplant, carefully marking front and rear positions on your mounts. Placing your engine in line with the marks, the next job is to precisely mark the positions of the mounting holes. To do this, I use a mechanical draftsman's pencil that allows the lead to be any length I wish. If you've no draftsman's pencil, simply cut a wood pencil to allow the lead to extend for about an inch. Scrub the point on a small piece of sandpaper and you have an accurate marking tool to reach down through the mounting holes on your engine.

You will see reference made to blind mounting nuts, normally in conjunction with the motor mounts. These are among the most

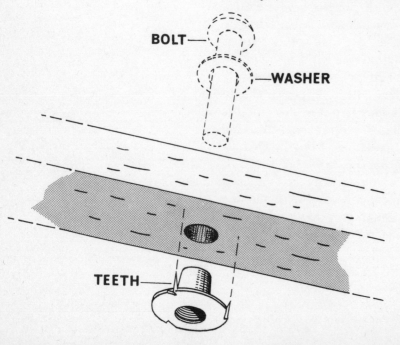

BOLT

WASHER

TEETH

Blind Mounting Nut seen here as used in a motor mount installation. A hole is drilled in the motor mount to receive the blind nut. The nut is pressed into the hole, and when the bolt is tightened, the teeth of the nut are drawn tightly into the wood, leaving the nut permanently mounted and locked in position; twist-free.

valuable items ever made as far as the modeler is concerned. However, be on the lookout for their location as you build because, if they're omitted, the structure must be disassembled in order to install them. The most commonly used nut and bolt in modeling is the 4-40 size, and the 4-40 blind mounting nut requires a ⅛-inch hole to fit into. With most smaller engines, and many of the larger ones too, the hole in the motor flange will be very close to the crankcase, allowing scant wood on the mount for the blind mounting nut to bite into. Drill the holes in the wood carefully. Enlarge them, if needed, with a round needle file; press the blind mounting nut into the hole, then place a washer on the other side of the mount; insert a bolt and draw the blind mounting nut up firmly into the hole. DON'T try to put the nut into the hole with the aid of a hammer—it will go off center, splinter the wood, and probably fail to do its function. Although the blind mounting nuts seldom work loose, it is best to smear them with epoxy for safety's sake, being careful not to fill the threads with epoxy. To be doubly sure that no epoxy gets into the threads, put the bolt into the nut, then epoxy the nut. Any overlap onto the bolt will only make for more threads and a stronger grip.

SHAPING OF FORMS. Even those with woodworking experience will often encounter some problems with the forming of shapes in balsa when they attempt their first carving and sanding. Balsa is light, pulpy, granular, stubborn, easy, hard, strong, and weak. Each piece is its own master, depending on how it was cut from the original log, but unlike other woods for which long hours are needed to obtain a shape, the worker using balsa obtains his in a relatively short time with far greater ease once he learns the quirks of the material. Many, sensing the softness and ease of working the material, will take a knife and try to cut through the balsa in one stroke. Too late, they learn that balsa doesn't respond to rough treatment or hasty methods. Slow, gentle slices work best, and with thick pieces (anything over ¹⁄₁₆ inch is thick in balsa!), it is best to make the cut with two or more passes with the blade over the same line. Trying to cut on one pass will result in splits and tears, no matter how sharp the blade. Obtaining rounded shapes is done in the same general manner. The piece to be formed, say a block that will make the nose of the plane, is first cut to a rough side outline with a coping or jigsaw, then the razor plane is put to work to gently shave the unit down to the other outline shape, as viewed from the top or bottom. Then the rounded corners are formed, again using the razor plane. The impatient will try to do it all quickly with the aid of a large knife, a sander, or a rasp. Unless one is experienced in working with this strange wood, one will be in trouble *fast!*

What happens if you remove too much wood by accident? Simple. Just plane a flat spot where the mistake was made, and

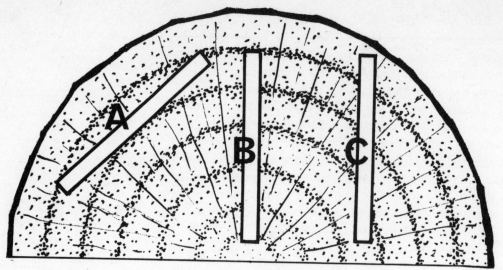

Cross section of balsa log

Balsa Identification Chart

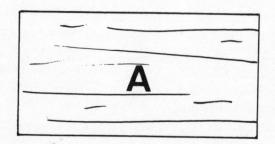

A-GRAIN sheet balsa has long fibers which show up as long grain lines. It is very flexible, bends around curves easily. Warps easily. Use for sheet covering rounded fuselages and wing leading edges, planking fuselages, forming tubes, strong flexible spars. Don't use for sheeting wings and tails, or flat fuselage sides, or formers.

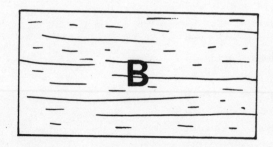

B-GRAIN sheet balsa has some of the qualities of both type A and type C. Grain lines are shorter than type A, and it feels stiffer across the sheet. It is a general-purpose sheet and can be used for many jobs. Use for flat fuselage sides (heavy duty), trailing edges, wing ribs, formers, planking gradual curves, wing leading-edge sheeting. Don't use it where type A or C will do a better job.

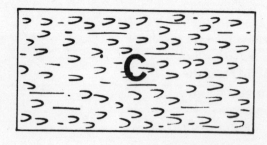

C-GRAIN sheet balsa has a beautiful mottled appearance. It is very stiff across the sheet and splits easily. But when used properly it builds the lightest strongest models. Use for sheet balsa wings and tails, flat fuselage sides (light duty), wing ribs, formers, sheet-covered leading edges with slight curves. Don't use for curved planking, rounded fuselages, round tubes (except indoor).

The strength of balsa is directly related to its density. The heavier the wood, the stronger and harder it is. Densities run from 5 to 20 pounds per cubic foot. Ten- to 12-pound balsa is considered medium weight. (Courtesy of Sig Mfg. Co.)

glue on a new piece, larger than that lost. Then carve the new piece to fit in with what you were originally trying to obtain in the way of shape.

Once the builder has the balsa shape reasonably close to the final form, he puts down the razor plane and uses sandpaper to do the finish shaping. Sandpaper, thus used, can be on a block, small pieces held in one's fingers, or even emery boards like women use to touch up their fingernails. These last have a million and one uses for the modeler, and I recommend your keeping a pack on your workbench.

Small forming tasks, such as shaping the leading edge of a wing, tail surfaces, and the like can best be done by using sandpaper on a block. The experienced builder can obtain the rough shape with the razor plane, but the beginner is better off going the sandpaper route, taking off a little wood at a time.

REPAIRING BUILDING DENTS. No matter how careful a builder may be, he will invariably suffer dents in the frame of his creation as he moves toward final covering. These always happen, even to the best of the international champions, and the repairs for such damage are quite simple. Fairly sizable dents in balsa may be removed by placing a damp cloth over the dented area and steaming the area with a hot iron. Holes that may have been caused by dropped tools, or other carelessness, can be filled with balsa scraps and then sanded down to the original contour. Minor holes can be filled and sanded down after an application of talcum powder mixed with dope to the consistency of a paste. This is best done by putting on a slight excess of the mix to allow for shrinkage. There are at present several commercially available balsa fillers, but to my liking, none have the same exact sanding or working qualities of balsa as does the talc-and-dope mixture.

CUTTING. Unless previously informed, the beginner will usually try to hack his way through all materials with a razor blade. While the razor blade is the most used item for a majority of cutting jobs, there are times when one needs other tools to do the task more efficiently, and one of these is the razor saw. Selling for under $2, these saws have a seemingly endless working life and are used to cut not only wood, but aluminum and brass tubing and some steel items such as small bolts. They are used solely for straight cuts, making a very fine cut hardly wider than a razor blade might make, but with a great deal more ease and accuracy.

Making long cuts across plywood (2 inches or longer) becomes difficult with a razor saw due to the fineness of the blade and teeth. For these longer cuts, and any cuts involving curves, a coping or jigsaw is used, the latter being the more preferable of the two in obtaining accurate cuts.

Balsa sheet over $1/16$ inch thick should be cut with either the razor saw or the coping or jig saw. Plywood over $\frac{1}{32}$ inch thick should be cut the same way. *Thin* metals and plastics may be cut with the razor saw, coping or jig saw, but thick metals should be cut with tin snips or a hacksaw. Thin means any material $\frac{1}{32}$ inch (.036) or less in thickness, and thick refers to any material $\frac{3}{64}$ inch (.048) and thicker. Plastics should be cut with a slow sawing motion, since heat from a fast moving blade will weld the material back together.

Wire used in modeling is predominantly that called "piano wire," a highly tempered steel wire that ranges in size from $\frac{1}{64}$ inch (.015) to $\frac{3}{16}$ inch (.300). Wire up to $\frac{1}{16}$ inch may be cut with wire-cutting pliers. Over $\frac{1}{16}$ inch this wire is cut by filing a notch at the point where the cut is desired, then snapping it in two and filing or grinding the snapped end smooth. These breaks often leave a very jagged, extremely sharp point on the wire that can be dangerous.

Cutting small, round holes, such as the points where dowel wing and tail holders are inserted into the fuselage, is quite simple with the aid of a 3-inch-long piece of brass tubing of the same diameter as the dowel to be used. The tubing is locked into the chuck of a power drill, and with the drill running, the end of the tubing is sharpened by holding sandpaper or emery cloth against it at a slight angle. When used as a hole cutter, it is placed in a small *hand* drill chuck and "drilled" in at the proper location. A power drill is *not* used. It is too hard to be accurate with a hand-held power drill.

Silk, nylon, and other lightweight fabrics are cut with either a razor blade or a pair of good shears bought and kept solely for this purpose. The razor blade, if used, should always be a new one, with cutting done on a pad of newspapers to allow the edge of the blade to stay sharper than if cutting over a hard surface. For ease of cutting these lightweight fabrics to general shape with a razor, tape them at the corners over the newspaper pad, lay the part to be covered on top of the fabric and cut around it, leaving an inch of extra material all around. This same method may be employed with the newer plastic type covering materials. (Also see Chapter 10, "Covering.")

The cutting of plastic foam as used for wings and other parts is done with a red hot wire maneuvered over pre-set templates. It is *not* something a beginner should become involved with, for several reasons, among them being the fact that cutting foam wings requires special equipment that is useless outside the hobby should one decide to go on to other things.

Plastic tubing such as that used for push rods and their guides is cut by slicing it with a razor blade. When epoxied in place and an angular cut is desired flush with a surface, such as where the tubing exits the fuselage, a razor plane does the neatest job, taking off small slices at a time until the tubing is almost flush with the wood. The final portion is removed with a sanding block or an emery board.

BONDING. This same type of plastic tubing, and all other parts made of plastic, nylon, fiberglass, and the like, should always be washed in detergent before using, to remove mold-releasing solution and other manufacturing "dirt"; otherwise it is virtually impossible to glue or epoxy them with any sort of lasting bond. Even with this washing, the parts to be bonded should first be roughened with sandpaper, file, or knife blade to insure a good grip for the adhesive, being sure to clean the filed, sanded, or scraped section before attempting to apply the bonding agent.

Wire rods to be joined to push rod tubing should be heavily abraded at the joining point with a file, cleaned with acetone, then dipped in epoxy and inserted in the detergent-washed (and thoroughly dried!) tubing. Once this has set, the wire and tubing are surface-coated at the exterior junction point with epoxy, the epoxy extending for ½ inch on both surfaces as further insurance against vibration loosening the bond.

Points where the control rod tubing is epoxied in the fuselage or wing panels should be given a second application of epoxy before final covering, or at least 24 hours after the initial application, again "feathering" the epoxy beyond the original coating. While you made sure the first coating of epoxy was adequate, this second is to be *positive!* Vibration is a mean enemy—fight him from the outset!

Another form of "bonding" concerns that of eliminating electrical "noise" in your airplane, and this is as vital as fighting vibration. These static charges, set up by metal-to-metal contacts humming happily from engine vibrations, can send false commands to a receiver and demolish an airplane for no apparent reason. If you *must* use a metal clevis pin (push rod connector), bond it to its mate (metal control arm, bellcrank, and the like) with a short length of highly flexible stranded wire. This is done by soldering one end of the wire to the metal clevis, and the other to the arm or bellcrank. This must be done at all metal-to-metal contacts in your airplane that have even the slightest degree of movement in their contact points. Slight movement by hand is a virtual symphony of metallic "buzz" when the engine is running!

SAFETY MOUNTINGS. While we all learn certain methods of making fastenings, we also have to forget their basic simplicities when we take up R/C. A screw, simply driven into wood, may hold a hundred pounds of suspended weight for years. The same screw, similarly mounted in a R/C plane may let go after 30 minutes' flight time, even though it supports nothing more than 1 ounce in weight. Yes—vibration again!

Therefore, regardless of what a certain set of plans may say, train yourself to certain rules regarding screws and bolts, nuts and wood mounts: They will *all* "buzz" loose unless you take steps to insure they do not! Where common wood screws are specified, and perhaps supplied, *throw them away!* In their place, use sheet metal or self-tapping screws of the same or a slightly larger size. Drill a hole for them of their center shaft size (shaft minus threads), then coat the screw with Magic Rubber or Silastic before screwing it into the drilled hole. This rubber coating will make it less apt to rotate free under engine vibrations.

Where bolts are used to secure parts, "safety" the nuts with Magic Rubber or Silastic for the same reason, being sure to clean nut *and* bolt with acetone in advance. These methods are used at *any* place where metal fasteners are used that may possibly work loose under the constant "buzz" of the ever-present vibration from the plane's engine—and this is everywhere!

Any place where metal is to be permanently affixed to the airframe (such as a tail wheel fitting), the metal should first be roughened, then cleaned with acetone before applying *epoxy*. Note the word *epoxy*. Other forms of modeling are able to use cement or glue to hold such parts—*don't* do it in R/C! Sizes, stresses, and weight loads are greater in R/C, and bonding should be similar in all cases to those used in full-scale aircraft.

METAL-TO-METAL. There are still instances in modern modeling where the builder must make solder joints, and if you've never worked with solder, take an hour or two to practice some of the requirements, *before* you try it on valuable parts.

First, there is of course the soldering iron, or "gun," with most builders preferring the latter. Since little if any soldering of electrical parts is any longer required, the small, relatively low-heat soldering irons are not required. Best all-around gun is the 250-watt size.

You will need solder, but do *not* use the *acid core* type. The most popular is an English resin core brand available at radio and TV supply shops. Called "Ersin," this solder melts at a relatively low temperature, is known as "60/40" (60 parts tin, and 40 parts lead), and has its own flux (antioxide) in five inner cores. A roll of this solder will last the average modeler for many, many years. (I've had a roll for over 12 years, and have used less than half of it—and that's with fixing a lot of broken household items!)

In spite of the solder having its own flux, results are far more satisfactory if you use extra flux, and a small tin of soldering paste, like the solder itself, seemingly lasts forever.

The iron is tinned according to the instructions supplied by the manufacturer, and kept clean by wiping, while hot, with a thick pad of clean rags.

Parts to be soldered are roughened with a file, or sandpaper, and then cleaned thoroughly with acetone. Soldering paste is then applied to the metal parts with aid of a small stick or length of small-diameter music wire, spreading a very thin, even coat of the paste where bonding is desired.

The gun is allowed to heat to its full capacity, then placed against the point to be soldered. The flux, or paste, will burn off quite quickly, but wait for the heat of the gun to heat the parts thoroughly, normally 15 to 30 seconds, before applying the solder. If the part is hot enough, the solder will flow into the joint and be in an entirely liquid state. Draw the gun away, and let the part cool. Do *not* disturb the solder joint for at least 15 seconds, otherwise you can end up with one of the R/C flyer's bugaboos—a "cold" solder joint, or one that seemingly holds, until vibration buzzes it loose, normally in the air, of course.

Some soldering, such as joining two wires, is done by first "tinning," or coating each wire with a thin layer of solder where the joint is desired, then placing the two wires together and touching them with the gun to melt the two together.

Where a wire or piece of tubing fits into another tube, the two are assembled, having first been cleaned and wiped with soldering paste; then the gun is applied to the outside rim of the larger tube where the smaller tube or wire enters it. Once hot, solder is applied at this point, and heat draws the solder up between the two, forming an inside bond.

One place that always gives the novice trouble is the soldering of washers that act as wheel retainers. He will normally get the washers soldered, perhaps burning the nylon wheel hub a bit, and then find that the wheel will not turn because the washers bind it in place. This is solved by punching a hole in a scrap of paper, slipping the paper over the axle next to the wheel, then putting the washer on next to the paper. After the washer is soldered, the paper is torn away, having protected the wheel from being burned. If binding still occurs, chances are it is an excess of flux that seeped into the wheel hub, and this may be removed with vinegar, or acetone if the wheel hub is not plastic. Acetone is very good for cleaning away excess flux once soldering is finished.

Although no longer in common usage, the wire landing gear made up of several pieces is occasionally called for. Joining these pieces is done by first wrapping the joints with fine wire, then soldering. Solder alone will not hold. On joints as large as these, a soldering gun is often inadequate to deliver enough heat to make a good joint. This is where the small, inexpensive blowtorch of the throw-away fuel can type come in handy. The joint is heated with the torch, then the solder is flowed on while the wire is still hot. Care must be taken not to get the wires red hot though, as this takes out the temper of the wire and makes it useless as a part of a landing gear.

Heat can cause other problems in soldering, too, burning up parts before the solder joint is completed. If a part to be soldered is near a part that looks as though it may burn, use a "heat sink." A heat sink is simply anything that will divert the heat of the gun, preventing it from traveling beyond where it is desired. You may purchase one at a radio-TV supply shop or make one from a piece of scrap aluminum or copper wire. If copper wire is used, care must be taken that it is kept away from the solder; otherwise it will stick fast. One way to make the copper wire safe from sticking onto the solder is to wipe it with a light coat of household oil. Wire used for this purpose would be the type found in common household wiring—one strand stripped of its insulation. This form of heat sink is simply placed, or secured, at a point next to the place to be soldered, in a position to divert heat from traveling to a delicate part.

Another highly satisfactory heat sink is the "alligator" clip, a small metal-jawed clip available in most hobby shops. This clip is preferred by many as the easiest of all to use in most applications.

Always test ALL solder joints in two ways: First, if the solder joint is bright and shiny, chances are it is good. One that is dull or wrinkled in appearance is probably a bad one, normally called a cold solder joint. This type is almost guaranteed to let loose under vibration. Second, give every solder joint a vigorous pull-and-twist test. Don't worry about abuse—if it lets go under these conditions, you can be well assured that it will let go much sooner under vibration. Better to fail in a simple test than in the air!

10
Covering

Lest you think that because you have an all-balsa plane covering is therefore not necessary, think back to the many mentions made concerning fuel and the damage it does, the ease of acquiring dents during building, and the need for strength in R/C planes.

Covering is important as a shield against fuel; properly applied it turns balsa wood into a tough material, and even tissue over balsa produces an almost unbelievable "skin" strength. (NOTE: Do not install hinges or fittings until covering is complete.)

There are several methods of covering a plane, ranging from the old standby, tissue and/or silk, to the latest space age heat-shrink plastics. For the builder who wants beauty in short order, or who has a wife or mother who gets ill at the smell of aircraft dope, the heat-shrink plastics are *the* answer.

This material, presently available in hobby shops under two brand names, "MonoKote" and "Solarfilm," each slightly different than the other, is applied to a model with a small iron, and also shrunken drum tight with the use of an ordinary household iron or the more exotic heat guns available at hobby shops. This covering and finish is all applied in an easy manner. Painting is not required and is in fact impossible. The use of these products is best described in the following reprint from *R/C Modeler Magazine:*

Solarfilm and Monokote Finishes

The introduction of Super MonoKote, manufactured and distributed in the U.S. by Top Flite Models, Inc., 2635 S.

Wabash Ave., Chicago, Illinois 60616, and the English Solarfilm, distributed in the United States by Pactra Corp., 6725 Sunset Blvd., Hollywood, California 90028, have virtually revolutionized the finishing of model aircraft. Basically, these are plastic films with an adhesive back wherein the color of the material is contained in the adhesive. With virtually every opaque, transparent, and metallic color available from Super MonoKote and Solarfilm, you can obtain a professional looking finish in a fraction of the time that it would normally take to finish by one of the more conventional methods such as dope, epoxy, or acrylic lacquer. All of the tedious work of sealing, doping, sanding, and polishing is eliminated while giving you a strong lightweight model that is fuel proof, moisture proof, stain proof and easy to maintain and repair.

Now, a few general observations about both of these materials. First of all, they are extremely light, since the total weight difference between a bare structure and a finished and trimmed airplane, such as the RCM Advanced Trainer, is 4 to 4½ ounces. The initial outlay for material is somewhat expensive, but not so when it is compared to the amount of dope, sanding sealer, color coats and miscellaneous material necessary to finish a model in the conventional painted manner. The materials stand up extremely well in the various weather conditions and are quite easy to work with once you understand and have practiced the techniques.

What is the difference between Super MonoKote and Solarfilm? Quite simply, the differences are slight and it's a "you pays your money and takes your choice" situation. Super MonoKote is slightly stronger than Solarfilm, thus provides more structural value to areas to where it is applied. Solarfilm, on the other hand, is slightly less strong but is substantially more flexible and easier to work around compound curves. Super MonoKote offers a better overall color coating, since Solarfilm often is not quite as opaque as Super MonoKote and the color coatings are not quite as even in some cases. Solarfilm, however, is much more puncture resistant than Super MonoKote and has more of a tendency to "give" rather than to rupture or tear. We have used both materials, extensively, and keep a supply of both on hand at all times. Both companies offer a wide range of colors, and, since the colors do differ from each other, you may find, for example,

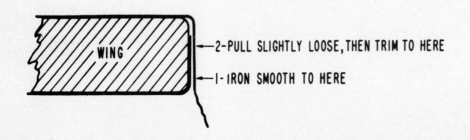

that you like Super MonoKote Transparent Yellow far better than the Solarfilm Transparent Yellow, while the Solarfilm Light Blue may appeal to you more than the comparable color in MonoKote. Since both can be used together, it is up to you to decide which material you like best and use that material according to the following techniques.

First of all, no dope, primer, or sealer of any kind is used on the surfaces of your model. When you apply MonoKote or Solarfilm, using heat, air gets trapped underneath. If the surfaces underneath are sealed with any type of material, this air cannot escape and you will end up with a bad job, little adherence of the material, and any dope that you have applied will blister with heat. Solarfilm, due to the lesser amount of heat required for adherence, can be applied over a doped surface, but it is entirely unnecessary and will not be discussed in this chapter. What is necessary, is that all surfaces to be covered have been sanded as smooth as you can possibly obtain them following the techniques illustrated at the beginning of this chapter. In other words, progressing from coarse to fine sand paper, sand the model as smooth as you can, filling all cracks, dinges, and gouges before you begin to apply the MonoKote or Solarfilm. Before you begin to apply the material to each section of the model, make sure that you have gone over the entire surface several times with a tack rag in order to eliminate all sanding residue and dust particles. If you do not do a thorough job at this point, the dust particles and sanding residue trapped between the surface of the model and the thin MonoKote or Solarfilm covering will stand out like a sore thumb on your finished model.

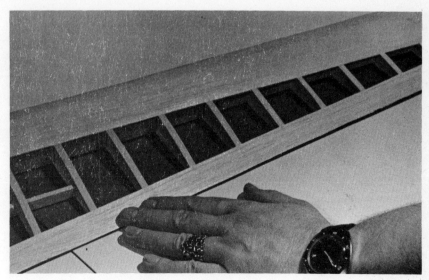

Before covering your model with Solarfilm, be certain that the framework of your model is sanded absolutely smooth and then dusted thoroughly with a tack cloth just before the covering material is applied.

Lay the wing panel out on a sheet of Solarfilm and cut off the amount needed allowing sufficient overlap all the way around the wing panel. The bottoms of both wing panels are covered first.

ABOVE: Cut away the amount of Solarfilm you plan to use on the wing panel, using a long straightedge and an X-Acto knife.
BELOW: Lay the cut-out piece of Solarfilm over the bottom wing panel and gently smooth out the excess wrinkles with the palm of your hand.

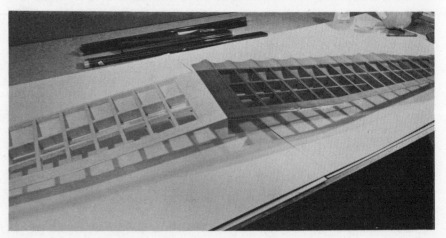

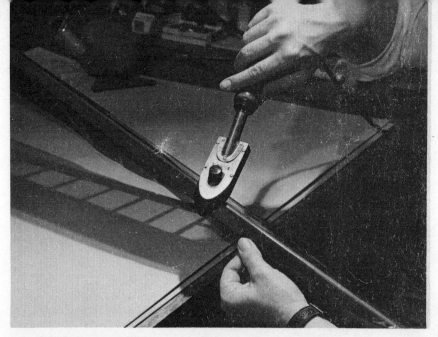

ABOVE: *Next, seal the leading edge of the wing, pulling the material down as you go to avoid any unsightly wrinkles.*
BELOW: *Seal the root and tip edges with your Sealectric iron.*

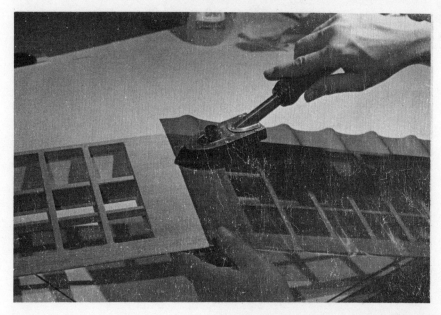

Seal trailing edge of the wing in the same fashion as you did the leading edge, pulling out any large wrinkles as you go, but do not attempt to pull the material drum tight.

Pull the material over the edge of the wing tip and you will find that your Sealectric iron goes around the compound curves quite easily.

Trim off the excess material along the leading edge of the wing, using your X-Acto knife.

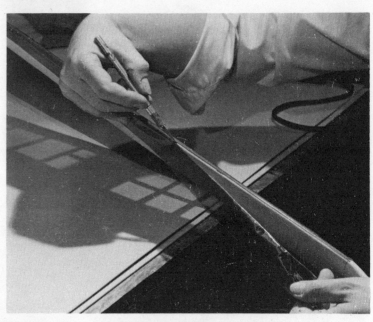

LEFT: Repeat the process for the trailing edge, cutting off the overhanging excess material.
BELOW: Reseal all edges around the trailing edge, wing center section, leading edge and tip. Now repeat the entire previous process for the bottom of the opposite wing panel.

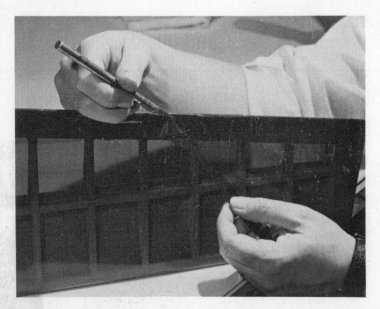

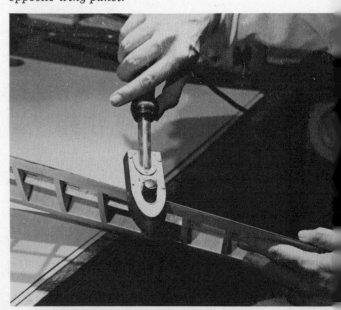

Cut a piece for the top of one wing panel and repeat the entire process for the top of both panels. Be sure to overlap the material at least ⅛ inch so that it bonds securely to the material on the lower side of the wing.

Before heat-shrinking the material, take a straight pin and poke a small hole at the junction of each rib in the trailing edge to allow the trapped air inside to escape and prevent bulging the material when it is heat shrunk.

LEFT: Take out major wrinkles by using your heat gun approximately 3–4 inches away from the material, moving it back and forth across one panel at a time.
BELOW: Do one or two bays at a time, reshrinking the material to the degree of tautness required.

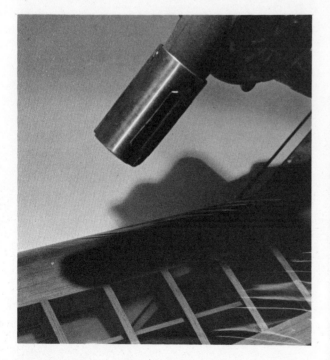

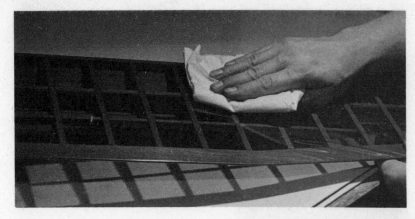

When you have completed one or two bays, and while the Solarfilm is still hot, rub the heated bays with a pad of Kleenex to make sure that the material adheres firmly to the wooden structure underneath. This will give you an excellent covering job that is absolutely scratch-free.

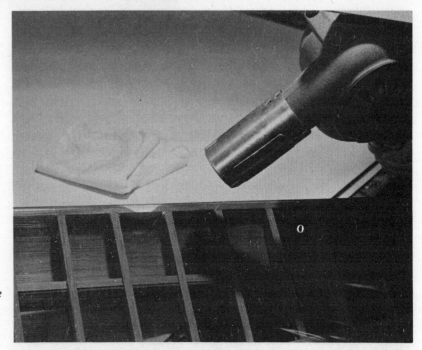

ABOVE: *An overdose of heat. What can happen if you hold the heat gun too close to the Solarfilm for too long a period of time.*

BELOW: *Covering a stabilizer is basically the same procedure as for a wing. Cut an oversized piece for half of the bottom panel first.*

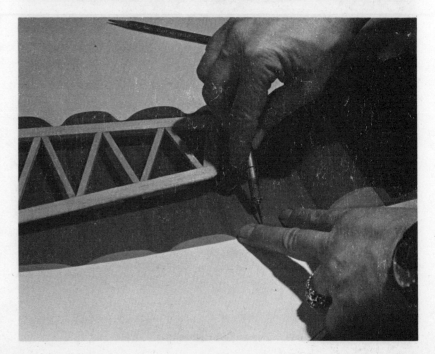

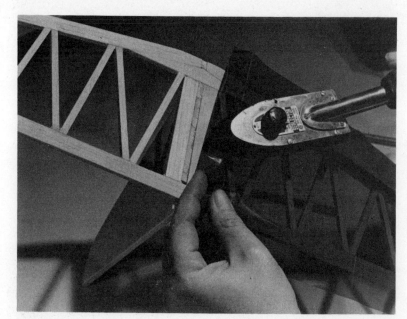

Seal the material at the center section using your Sealectric iron.

Seal the leading and trailing edges, pulling out the heavier wrinkles as you go.

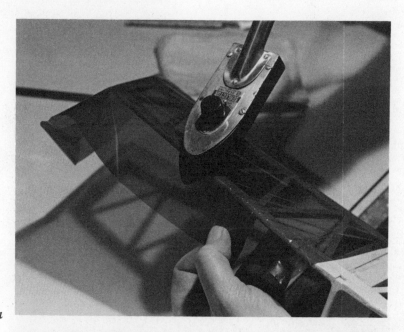

Heat the material around the back of the trailing edge of the stabilizer so that you will have a good overlap when the top covering is applied.

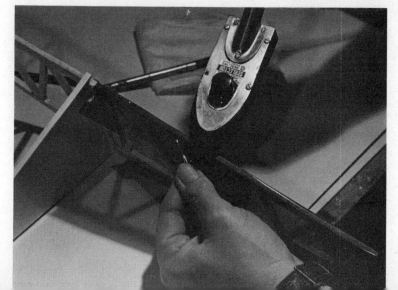

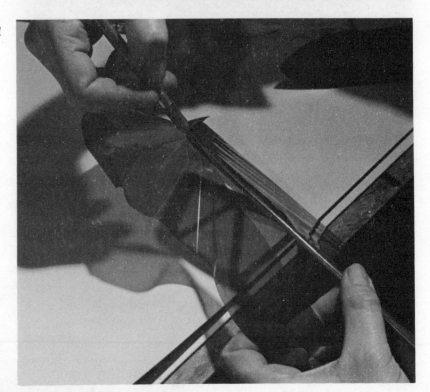

ABOVE: *Cover the compound curve of the stabilizer tip in the same fashion as you did the wing.*

BELOW: *Remove all excess material from around the leading edge, trailing edge and tip.*

Reseal all of the edges once again, and then proceed with the other half of the stab bottom, followed by each half of the stabilizer top.

Since you have eliminated a lot of elbow grease necessary in the application of dope and sanding sealer on a conventional finish, take a little extra time at this point to do a good job of surface preparation before beginning the actual application of the material.

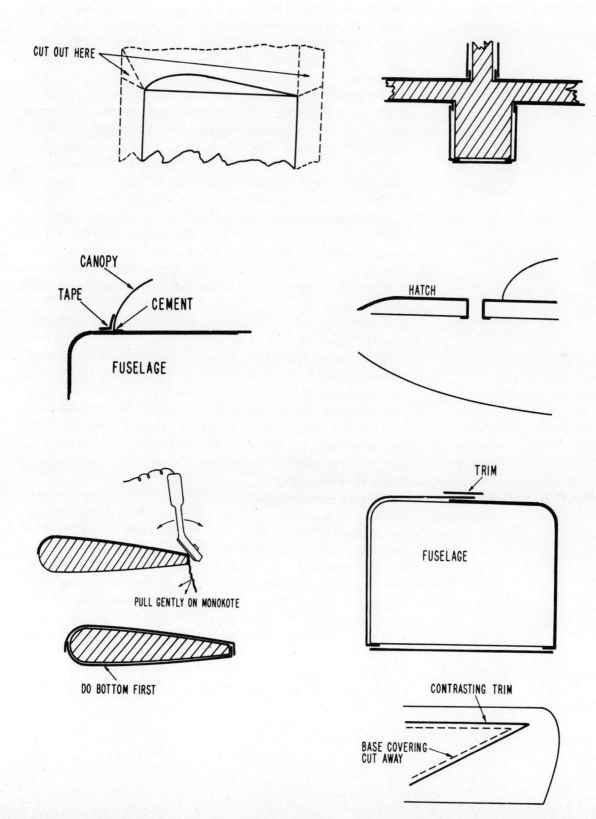

CUT OUT HERE

CANOPY

TAPE

CEMENT

FUSELAGE

HATCH

PULL GENTLY ON MONOKOTE

DO BOTTOM FIRST

TRIM

FUSELAGE

CONTRASTING TRIM

BASE COVERING
CUT AWAY

The tools that you will need for applying Super MonoKote or Solarfilm is a heat gun, such as the Polytherm or AME heat guns, which put out approximately 300–400 degrees of heat, and a Sealectric electric iron available through most hobby shops for the application of these materials. The latter is a small tacking iron which is used in photography to seal photographic prints to cardboard backing frames as well as in butcher shops to heat seal meat packages. The best "shoe" that we have discovered for use with the Sealectric iron is the new Super Shoe from Robart Mfg., P.O. Box 122, Wheaton, Ill. 60187. This Super Shoe simply replaces the one that comes on your Sealectric iron and is more advantageous due to its double tapered tip, allowing you to get into corners such as the junction between the fin and the stabilizer much more easily than the standard shoe supplied with the Sealectric iron. The Robart Super Shoe has a generous coating of tough Teflon "S" and, given reasonable care, this coating will provide many years of service to you.

Start covering your trainer by doing the primary flight surfaces first, such as the rudder and elevator, in order to learn the techniques of applying this type of material. Place a sheet of Super MonoKote or Solarfilm on a table and lay the part to be covered on it. Cut the panel of the covering material approximately one inch larger chordwise and 2″ or longer than the length of the panel. Whenever you are covering wings, stabilizers, and elevators, it is recommended that the bottom be covered first.

Remove the Super MonoKote or Solarfilm from its backing sheet and lay on the part to be covered, adhesive side down. If you cannot determine which side has the adhesive, touch the iron point to the edge of the material. The iron will stick only to the adhesive side. Be sure to allow at least one-half inch overlap all around. We do not recommend "wrapping" the material around the piece to be covered, but use one piece to cover each side.

Setting your Sealectric iron at its hottest temperature setting for either material, tack down all four sides or edges of silkspan when covering an open structure. Since the material shrinks when heat is applied it takes a little patience to do this neatly. Try to gently tighten the material as you do this operation, getting it as smooth as possible, using your Sealectric iron. Remember, you are using one piece for the top surface and one piece for the bottom, which means that the two will have to overlap. For minimum seam visibility, cover the bottom surfaces first.

After you have one panel tacked down all around the edges, use your electric heat gun and a pad of several layers of Kleenex to shrink the material. This process is quite simple and is illustrated in the photographs. By applying heat to a small area at a time, that area will shrink up tight and it is immediately rubbed down with the pad of Kleenex so that the adhesive, which has become tacky from the applied heat, will adhere the material to the balsa surface. If the material is not adhered to the surface, no structural value of any kind will be gained from the covering material. By using the heat gun and the pad of Kleenex, instead of the iron, you will eliminate all scratches and mars that the iron would otherwise put on the surface of the material. Do a small section at a time until you finish the section to be covered. When you get near the end of a sheeted surface, trapped air and heat will cause the material to bubble and you will have difficulty making it adhere. Simply prick the bubbles with the end of a pin, then reheat and rub down with the pad of Kleenex. Do this as often as necessary and you will obtain a smooth wrinkle-free surface. The pin holes will not show once the material has been completely sealed to the wood. When you get to the rounded tips of your rudder and elevator, and particularly on the compound curves of a wing tip, you will find out how really good this material is. By patiently heating, pulling, and reheating it will go completely around compound curves and, miraculously, the adhesive (and color) does not separate from the mylar base even with repeated reheatings. There is also very little bleed of the liquefied adhesive. In fact, any of the adhesive that remains can be wiped off with alcohol or lacquer thinner [also acetone]. You can obtain a smoother wing tip by working the material further around than intended, then pulling slightly loose and trimming where originally planned, following by sealing the edge down again.

By the way, when sealing overlapped edges with a small iron, use a little pressure. A tiny little bit of gooey adhesive that seeps out can later be removed with a rag dampened with dope or lacquer thinner [or acetone]. You will find that, by this method, seams are almost invisible. In order to trim overlapped materials so that the slightly visible seam will be straight, apply a straight guide line with ¼″ wide masking tape on the unwanted portion of material. Use the masking tape and the unwanted material and tape will be removed leaving you with an absolutely straight seam.

After you have finished the rudder, elevator, etc., do the wing next. Even if you have a perfectly straight wing with no dihedral, no sweep or taper, use four pieces of MonoKote or Solarfilm: a top and a bottom piece for each wing half with a lap in the dihedral joint. The process for the wing is to cover the bottom panels first followed by the top panels overlapping on the trailing edge and making your overlap on the bottom side of the wing just past the front of the leading edge. Start the wing by tacking down from the center of the leading edge out to each end and from the center of the trailing edge out to each end. Seal the material at the center section and at the last wing rib. Now, doing a small section at a time, follow the same procedure as previously outlined using the heat gun and Kleenex pad until all wrinkles have been removed from the wing covering, the drum material is tight, and completely adhered to the ribs and leading and trailing edge sheeting. Now, trim off all excess material from the center section and leading and trailing edge leaving an overhang in material for the compound curve of the tip. To finish the tip, pull the excess material while applying the heat to the surface. The heat will make it pliable so that it may be pulled out over the tip using the point of the small iron. Repeat this process every inch or so along the tip until the tip has been completely sealed, and then, and only then, use the electric heat gun and Kleenex pad to finish out all wrinkles in the material. Be absolutely certain that you do not apply the heat from the heat gun too close to the material or you will melt a hole directly through it! If this happens, you can either patch the area or alternately, completely remove the covering from the panel and start over again. It is much easier to apply too little, and increase the amount of time the heat is applied to a given area, than to try to come too close and apply too much heat at once, causing the material to pull away or, even worse, to melt completely through the material.

When covering the stabilizer, first do the bottom, then the top of the stabilizer with an overlap on the fuselage and rudder. As for the fuselage, you can do the top and bottom followed by the two sides or you can use two pieces with a joint down the center on the top and the bottom of the fuselage covering the joint with a contrasting piece of trim material. If there is a hatch, cover separately as shown in the sketch, otherwise the edges would eventually lift. Inside the engine compartment where it could be almost impossible to do a neat job, finish (and fuelproof at the same time) with either matching color dope or Hobbypoxy paint. You will find that Hobbypoxy stock color matches Super Mono-Kote almost perfectly while a combination of Hobbypoxy paint and Aerogloss dope will match the various colors of Solarfilm.

The final step is putting on the trim. We have found that the best way to do this is to use the MonoKote Regular Trim

Sheets which are available in virtually every color of the rainbow and available at almost all hobby shops throughout the country. Trace out the outline of the trim [see Chapter 11, "Color Trim"] you want to use on the back of the backing sheet which is conveniently ruled off in guidelines for you. In addition, letters and numbers are marked on the back of the sheet so that you can apply your AMA number quite easily. This material is simply applied directly over the Super MonoKote or Solarfilm base color and smoothed out until no bubbles remain. The edges can be sealed with a very light application of low heat from your small iron or a "distant" application of low heat from your electric heat gun and the Kleenex pad. Solarfilm can be applied as trim by using the Solarfilm solvent which is available from dealers carrying this product. This is an oily type solvent which is wiped very lightly on the adhesive side of the Solarfilm, allowing the solvent to become sticky and permitting you to place the trim wherever you want it to go on your model. The only disadvantage with using this material over the MonoKote trim sheets is that it is virtually impossible to remove all the trapped air bubbles from between the two materials. Thus, we have used Monokote Regular Trim Sheets almost exclusively for trimming the material.

If you are applying large areas of trim such as a contrasting color to a wing, it is easier to remove the base covering if you have a fully sheeted wing, then apply contrasting trim about $\frac{1}{2}''$ larger all the way around than the material that you have removed. If you do not cut the base color away on large areas, the air trapped between the two layers cannot escape and the result will be large bubbles and wrinkles. For a large area such as this, where the base coat has been removed, you can use the Super MonoKote and the Solarfilm rather than the trim sheets, the latter being designed for application of trim to smaller areas only.

If you are building a model that requires a canopy such as a low wing competition multi, the installation of the canopy can be a problem. Fit the canopy to the fuselage; then trace the outline of the canopy on the MonoKote or Solarfilm with a sharp pencil. Cut away this material, completely exposing the balsa wood, and use the cut away portion as a pattern for cutting a smaller piece ($\frac{1}{16}''$ smaller around the entire circumference of the material) and use this to cut out an inner piece from flat black Contact Shelf paper. Apply this to the balsa wood area from which you previously removed the MonoKote or Solarfilm. This will leave a $\frac{1}{16}''$ bare balsa wood strip all the way around where the canopy will rest on the fuselage. Now you can apply standard DuPont

Plastic Cement to adhere the canopy to the balsa wood or, alternately, a product called Bond, available at most craft shops, has been found to hold canopies better than any adhesive yet discovered. This is not an easy-to-find material, but with a little diligence you should be able to find it at a local craft shop.

Finally, you can apply a piece of tape or MonoKote or Solarfilm all around the perimeter of the canopy to give a nice clean trim to the canopy-fuselage joint. If, at any time, you have to remove the applied covering, the adhesive residue can be removed from the balsa with a cloth moistened with acrylic lacquer thinner or acetone.

As with any other type of finish, the application of Super MonoKote or Solarfilm takes practice, patience, and more practice. Your final reward will come when you have applied this material to several aircraft, become completely familiar with its peculiarities, and have fully developed your application techniques. At that point, when another modeler walks up to you and asks you what you painted your model with, you will know that you have achieved the end result . . . a perfectly finished model that is easy to maintain and repair and can compare with the best applied paint finish with far less time and elbow grease required!

(Courtesy, *R/C Modeler Magazine*)

The die-hard purists, who still insist a wooden plane be covered with fabric, are highly disdainful of these plastic coverings and use instead silk, nylon, or various similar materials. To cover with these materials, the frame where the fabric is to adhere must first be given two coats of clear dope, sanding after each coat. The fabric is then applied, either wet or dry, using clear dope as the adhesive. If applied dry, the fabric is then sprayed with water to shrink it tight.

With the fabric thoroughly dry, dope is applied in successive light coats to further tighten the material, and after the fourth coat, a filler is applied, the filler being a commercially available one, or one made by adding talcum powder to dope. This filler fills in the weave of the fabric and makes for a better final finish. It is sanded with wet or dry paper, used wet; another coat of filler is applied if the weave is still visible, and the wet sanding repeated. Another coat of clear, more wet sanding, and then the color coat goes on and is wet sanded. If the color coat is not even in tone, another is applied and again wet sanded. When the color coat is satisfactory, a coat or two of clear is applied over the color, and the plane is rubbed down with rubbing compound and given a coat or two of wax. You are now perhaps more aware of why the plastic coverings have become so popular. However, when you have enough flying experience, and choose to try your hand at scale models, fabric *is* the required covering in many instances. After all, when you think about it, there just weren't too many plastic-covered Spads in World War I.

Needing less work than fabric covering, but not as simple as the plastic, is tissue. By "tissue," I do not mean just any old gift wrap variety, but, in the jargon of R/C, a specific paper called "silk-span," a material used in the making of tea bags. It is tough, purportedly made from bamboo fibers; lighter weights are called silkspan while heavier weights are called, strangely enough, "bamboo paper." It is lightweight and has enough shrink factor to make it ideally suited for modeling. Using it requires a part of the technique of using fabric, such as doping the frame, applying the covering wet or dry, wetting to shrink, and sanding lightly a couple of times with wet or dry sandpaper, used wet. But there is far less dope and effort expended to achieve a perfect finish because the silkspan accepts dope and fills in more rapidly than silk or nylon. While it does not offer the strength of fabric, it is quite close, and many scale modelers have forgotten its use, or have never been exposed to it at all. Put it on your list of things to try someday.

While there are many claims to the contrary, the use of the fabric or tissue covering methods *is* cheaper than the plastic coverings unless you count your time in application as a part of the price, and that's hardly fair when you consider that this *is* a hobby.

If you buy everything needed for a fabric or tissue covering job over the counter in a hobby shop, you will come out somewhere near the same price as the plastic materials. However, a part of this hobby in the eyes of many, is to see how much can be done for how little. On this note, should you choose to go the more laborious, but more economical route, buy your dope at the local airport, and *not* at the hobby shop. While it is very wise to support your local hobby shop in order to have a nearby supply of goodies, you can be selfish at times and think of yourself too. Dope purchased at hobby shops will cost more than quadruple what it will cost at the airport. An example: Randolph dope (one of the best), available in quarts (bulk if you wish), will make almost four quarts when cut with thinner; and the thinner used may be acetone, available at under $2 a gallon. Randolph dope is butyrate and as fuelproof as the already thinned down dopes sold in hobby shops.

(NOTE: This is no attempt to cut the hobby shops or the paint packagers out of the picture. The above is mentioned only to help those who may be working on limited funds.)

If you choose to forego the plastic coverings and try silk or tissue, the technique of covering is relatively simple. As mentioned previously the frame is given two coats of clear dope at all places where adhesion of the material is desired. On a wing, this will be all around the edges, normally doping a strip about an inch wide front and rear, top and bottom, around the tips, and a 2-inch-wide strip where the wing panels join. Do *not* dope the ribs! Tail surfaces are done like the wing, doping ½-inch-wide areas around all edges on both sides. The fuselage, if of all-balsa construction, is completely doped. If the fuselage is of built-up construction, and not covered with balsa, only the four main longerons are doped, along with the tail post and forward sheeted areas. Sand the dope between coats and be sure all is smooth and dust-free before going to the next step.

Place the wing down on the covering material and cut enough to do one panel, leaving an inch of extra material all around the panel, including tip and center section joint. Next, dunk the material (this includes tissue) in a bowl of clean water and *gently* squeeze out the excess water. Do *not* wring, and do not squeeze so hard as to form wrinkles or creases in the material.

Place the wet material in position over the wing panel and carefully pull it into a relatively tight condition (the water will hold it in place). Once the material is smoothed out you are ready to dope it to the wing. Do this with a fairly good-sized brush, a No. 8 round or ½- to ¾-inch flat, applying the dope starting at the center section, 6 inches to one side, then 6 inches to the side immediately opposite. The dope is brushed on *top* of the material, and both thumbs are then used to straighten and fasten the material by pressing down while pushing the material out toward the edges.

The material is likewise fastened at the center joint and wing-tip, pulling it taut with thumbs pressing it down into the dope. The rest of the materal is now fastened down in the same manner, doing 6 inches at a time on both edges until the material has been doped all the way around.

If a wrinkle develops, don't despair. Simply loosen the material by soaking with thinner and press and pull until the wrinkle is removed. As you pull the material up tight, be careful not to pull so hard that you twist the framework. The material still has to dry, and it will shrink during the drying. If you have too much tension at one point, the frame will twist as the material dries.

The rest of the model is covered in the same manner, with curves being covered in stages, using small pieces of material for each stage and overlapping each piece on the one previously applied. Always overlap the material about ⅛ inch and rub these overlaps with dope on your fingers to form a smooth, tight joint.

Whether silk, nylon, or tissue, use *sharp* scissors to cut the shapes from the large pieces and a *new* razor blade to do the final trimming of material on the frame after the dope has dried.

You may wonder why it was necessary to put two coats of dope on all edges of the frame. These coats soften as you apply dope on top of the material and give the surface dope a better grip. Trying to apply covering of this type without the two undercoats is virtually impossible. For this same reason, the ribs and other inner framing are left undoped so the later coats of dope on the material will not stick to them and cause uneven pulling as the material continues to tighten. Some builders insure ribs and framing remaining unstuck by waxing them before covering. A candle or a child's crayon work well for this protective coating.

Thin dope is used for the first few coats on silk and nylon in order to avoid drops of dope working through the fabric and drying in globs inside. These globs remain in spite of all efforts to remove them and shine stubbornly through, even on the final paint job.

With either silk, nylon, or tissue, a condition is likely to occur that makes you wonder what has gone flooey in your doping process. This is when whitish patches, called "blushing," appear and stay. These are caused by moisture trapped in the dope, and before you tear the covering off in disgust, brush it or spray it with thinner. Silver polish, briskly rubbed, will also relieve the condition. Putting more dope on top will *not*. To avoid it in the first place, don't dope on rainy or highly humid days.

If you choose spray paint, and have never done spray painting, do it in short bursts of spray, applying the paint much as though using a brush, with 10 to 12 inches being the longest distance covered by a burst. Use several thin coats, rather than one thick one in order to avoid drips.

Another word of caution about doping. Whether spraying or brushing, do so only with adequate ventilation. If using indoors in the winter, go no longer than 10 minutes before opening windows and completely airing the room. Dope is safe if used with common sense, but can cause severe brain and heart damage if used carelessly.

By the way, you may now install those hinges and fittings. To have them in sooner would mean working around them, or they would become full of paint and inoperable.

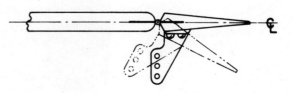

Cutaway sketch of control surface with hinge and control horn installed. Note that holes in horn are at right angles to hinge line when the surface is at the level position.

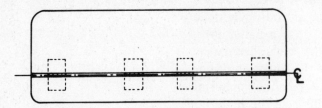

Alignment of hinge center lines in relationship to each other is important to avoid binding of control surfaces.

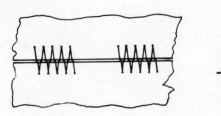

A hinge made of stitched nylon fishing line. The line is stitched over and under the surfaces in a figure eight pattern. A drop of cement is used at each point the line enters a surface. An excellent hinging method that guarantees no binding.

CREASED ON
CENTERLINE

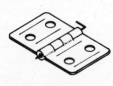

LEAF AND PIN
TYPE HINGE

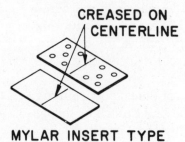

MYLAR INSERT TYPE

Use an X-Acto knife and a No. 11 blade with blade guide to cut hinge slots.

The IM small hinge, shown here, is made in Japan and is available in several sizes.

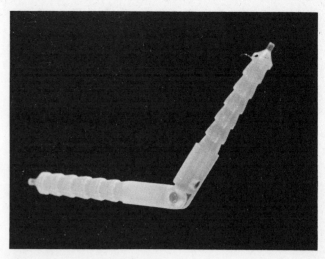

The Robart Hinge is used for control surfaces ³⁄₁₆″ or thicker.

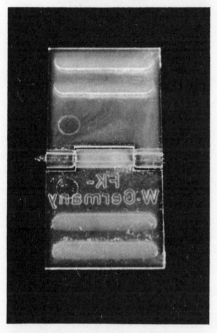

A relatively new hinge is the FK, manufactured in West Germany.

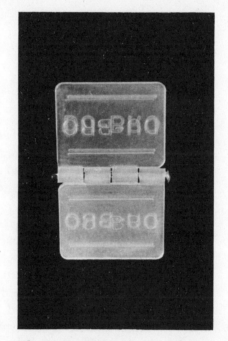

The Du-Bro Hinge is one of the mostly widely used.

The very popular Klett Hinge is available in two sizes.

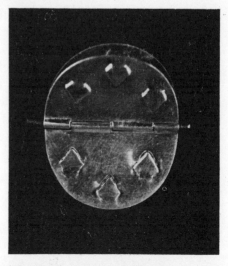

The Tatone Hinge, unlike the others, is made of metal.

11
Color Trim

Part of the enjoyment of modeling comes from the beauty of the finished model and the admiring glances one's creation receives from others. If you've had art or design training, you know how to go about trimming your model to give it eye appeal. If not, the following may help you.

The first consideration when choosing a color scheme, is to imagine the model in several circumstances: the ideal blue sky; the more often hazy sky; as seen against distant trees or mountains; and, sadly, as lost in a field of grass or corn. To this list, add the fact that you will need to know if the plane is coming toward you or going away, and, is it upside down or right side up? Obviously there is more to think of than a few little stripes and numbers.

First of all—visibility. You may feel that because your plane has a 5- or 6-foot wingspan, you will certainly have no trouble seeing it. Right? Wrong! A six-foot player, 100 yards away on a football field doesn't look too big—and he's bulked out with gaggles of pads and weighs over 200 pounds. Your model is a lot slimmer, especially if viewed from the side or, worse yet, from head on. One hundred yards is not the normal distance from which a modeler views his airborne plane either, especially a beginner. The beginner's ship will often be a quarter of a mile away before he summons the courage to try another turn to bring it back. So, planning the color scheme and trim can be very important!

Visibility of a model under all circumstances requires some simple planning. First a dominant color must be selected, one that will make up the bulk of color on the plane. Which color offers the greatest degree of visibility? If you guessed red, you are absolutely *wrong*. Don't feel bad, most people think red is a real attention grabber. On a woman, yes, but on planes, cars, fire engines, signs, and the like, *no!* Red has the same color scale value as green—the color of that grass or cornfield your plane could get lost in. Red planes almost literally disappear in such surroundings. If you doubt this, drop a small red object on a grass lawn and walk away from it. After 25 or 30 feet, turn around and see if you can spot it. Also try this with green, blue, maroon, black, gray, violet, brown.

Next, drop a white or yellow object. Whammo! Instant find! Orange too is good, but lower in light reflective qualities than yellow, and far lower than white, the brightest of them all.

So, knowing that white is the brightest of all pigments, we'll paint the whole thing white, add the numbers, and go flying! Wrong again. Let's put the plane up into a hazy sky. Out of sight in no time at all, so obviously we erred somehow. White is our champion, but we need to add something for those other occasions, such as the hazy day. For this we need some color deep on the color scale, such as black, brown, or even red, in addition to the white.

OK, you say, but where do we put what, and how do we put it to make the whole plane look good, as well as keeping it highly visible? First one must decide on the proportions of his color scheme, and the one I offer those who ask is a rule of Chinese art —"one man, one mountain, one sky." Translated from the Chinese, this means very simply that "man" (one color used) would be the very smallest, "mountain" (another color used) would occupy perhaps a third of the area, and "sky" (the third color used) would represent two-thirds of the entire color scheme. This gives a pleasant balance of colors to make for a pleasing color scheme, but we still have not decided on *what* colors, or how to place them.

Knowing that white is our highest reflective color, with yellow a close second, we then choose one of these as the color to paint (or cover) the entire airplane. (If yellow paint is chosen, put on a coat or two of white first to act as a base for the yellow, otherwise the yellow will never seem to be yellow, only a yellow green. If you're using the plastic type of covering, ignore this and go straight to yellow covering.)

With white as a total neutral, *any* colors may be used with it. Yellow is quite near to being a neutral, but as a primary color it loses "snap" when used with its neighbors on the color wheel, orange or green, both of which are made with the use of yellow

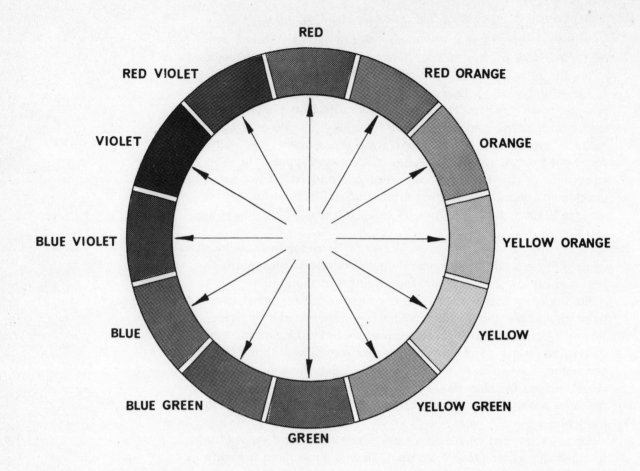

RED

RED VIOLET   RED ORANGE

VIOLET   ORANGE

BLUE VIOLET   YELLOW ORANGE

BLUE   YELLOW

BLUE GREEN   YELLOW GREEN

GREEN

Colors. This gray version of colors on the "colorwheel," shows them in their approximate color value to each other as seen by the camera's eye. Using any color across the wheel from another color is the best way to decide a color scheme, as long as the values (darkness or lightness) are in good contrast to each other. Easiest contrasts to recognize in this version are "yellow-violet." (See color chart for more examples.) If in doubt, separate all colors with white.

and another color. However, if the yellow is separated from the orange or green with white, each becomes quite vivid again. The safe rule of thumb for those doubtful of colors is always to separate *all* colors with white. An example of this is to view various planes that others have built and trimmed and to carefully observe signs and other roadside material as you travel about, even in your own community. Armed with the knowledge that white is the winner in high visibility and that other colors often conflict with each other, you'll begin to see some pretty vivid examples of both. If you live in a rural area you will more than likely see a homemade sign or two that is almost impossible to read because of the colors chosen by its creator—orange on blue, red on green, or *vice versa*. The words will seem to "vibrate" and hurt your eyes. This is because the colors chosen are of the same, or almost same, "value" on the color scale. To understand this fully, think of a black-and-white photo and how it "sees" color. It ignores the colors and sees all in shades of gray. If two colors, say orange and blue, are of the same value, they will photograph as the same shade of gray in a black-and-white photo, and this is why they tend to vibrate when seen with the human eye: Their values are identical and therefore fight for attention.

Try this experiment with the colors you choose for your plane. Place a chip of each color together on a gray surface (NEVER white!). Do they vibrate or hurt your eyes to look at? If so, choose a darker shade of one color, and try it with the other. Place white between the colors and note the new life the colors take on.

Let's look at some specific color schemes for those too puzzled by all this talk of values, areas, and so forth:

Basic ⅔ Color of Plane	⅓ of Color	Final Trim
White*	Orange	Black
White	Orange	Deep Blue Green
White	Orange	Deep Blue
White	Orange	Olive
White	Orange	Deep Green
		Deep Green
White	Orange	Deep Purple
White	Orange	Brown
White	Orange	Dark Gray
White	Orange	Maroon
White	Yellow	Black
White	Yellow	Deep Blue Green
White	Yellow	Deep Blue
White	Yellow	Olive
White	Yellow	Dark Gray
White	Yellow	Deep Purple
White	Yellow	Brown
White	Yellow	Dark Gray
White	Yellow	Maroon

* All colors are *separated* by white.

Basic ⅔ Color of Plane	⅓ of Color	Final Trim
White	Red	Black
White	Red	Deep Olive Green
White	Red	Deep Purple
White	Red	Dark Gray
White	Red	Gray
White	Medium Blue	Black
White	Medium Blue	Deep Olive Green
White	Medium Blue	Medium Red Violet
White	Medium Blue	Deep Purple
White	Medium Blue	Dark Gray
White	Medium Blue	Maroon
White	Medium Blue	Dark Brown
White	Yellow Green	Black
White	Yellow Green	Deep Olive Green
White	Yellow Green	Deep Purple
White	Yellow Green	Dark Gray
White	Yellow Green	Maroon
White	Yellow Green	Dark Brown
White	Yellow Green	Red Violet
White	Yellow Green	Orange
White	Yellow Green	Deep Blue Green
White	Yellow Green	Deep Blue
White	Blue Green	Black
White	Blue Green	Deep Olive Green
White	Blue Green	Deep Purple
White	Blue Green	Deep Gray
White	Blue Green	Maroon
White	Blue Green	Dark Brown
White	Blue Green	Dark Red Violet
White	Deep Blue Green	Orange
White	Light Blue Green	Deep Blue
Yellow	Red	Black
Yellow	Brown	Black
Yellow	Olive	Black
Yellow	Medium Green	Black
Yellow	Medium Gray	Black
Yellow	White	Black
Yellow	White	Dark Gray
Yellow	White	Orange
Yellow	White	Red

Basic ⅔ Color of Plane	⅓ of Color	Final Trim
Yellow	White	Brown
Yellow	White	Deep Blue
Yellow	White	Purple
Yellow	White	Olive
Red	White	Black
Red	White	Deep Blue
Red	White	Deep Olive
Red	White	Deep Purple
Red	White	Dark Gray
Red	White	Dark Brown
Orange	White	Purple
Orange	White	Black
Orange	White	Deep Blue
Orange	White	Dark Gray
Orange	White	Brown
Orange	White	Olive
Orange	White	Deep Blue Green
Orange	White	Magenta

Now let's put all this to work and figure out a color plan for your plane. As the sketches indicate, the planning of color areas is done by repeating lines of the plane's shape and repeating them in large and small areas. To plan your color scheme, do as I have done and make small sketches of your plane. Then, using color pencils, fill in the areas and see what it all looks like before trying it out on the actual model. Be sure to make a sketch of top and bottom, and, as I've done, make each entirely different so that when your plane is in the air, dead overhead, you will know whether it's upside down or right side up. If all this sketching and coloring is beyond you, copy the color scheme of a full-size plane or a model that appeals to you. In applying the trim, if you use paint, start with the lightest color; for example, if white is the lightest color in your paint scheme, paint the entire plane white, then add the other colors, and end with the darkest. Use masking tape to lay out areas and be sure to seal the edges toward the area to be painted with clear dope so that the color will not seep under the tape during doping.

Numbers and letters, if properly chosen, make an attractive

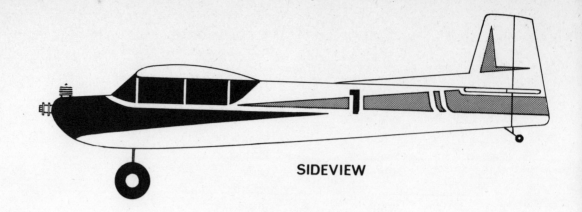

SIDEVIEW

Trim design. Note that in these sketches one color (represented by black) is dominant and that the second color (represented by gray) is secondary in size and importance. Also note that outlines of the plane are used to draw parallel lines to form the design areas and that top and bottom designs differ for clarity in the air. Make small doodles like this to establish your plane's trim before beginning to paint or mark.

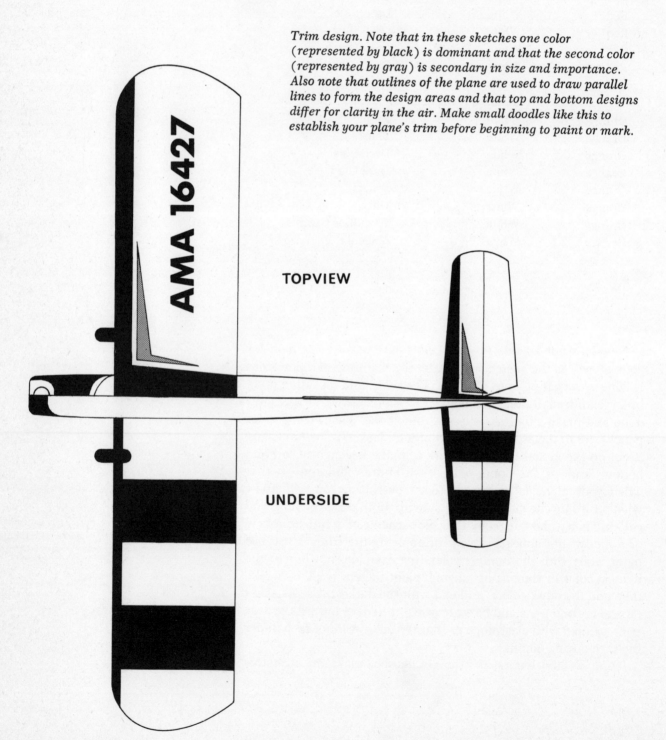

TOPVIEW

UNDERSIDE

AMA 16427

addition to a color scheme and should be planned as a part of it. The mistake most commonly made by many modelers is the use of letters and numbers that are too small. The illustration shows a typical Academy of Model Aeronautics license number, which is one-third of the wing chord, or the distance between leading and trailing edges of the wing. Small letters will look good only if incorporated into the overall design, as shown, but if you have doubts about your design abilities, use the larger letters.

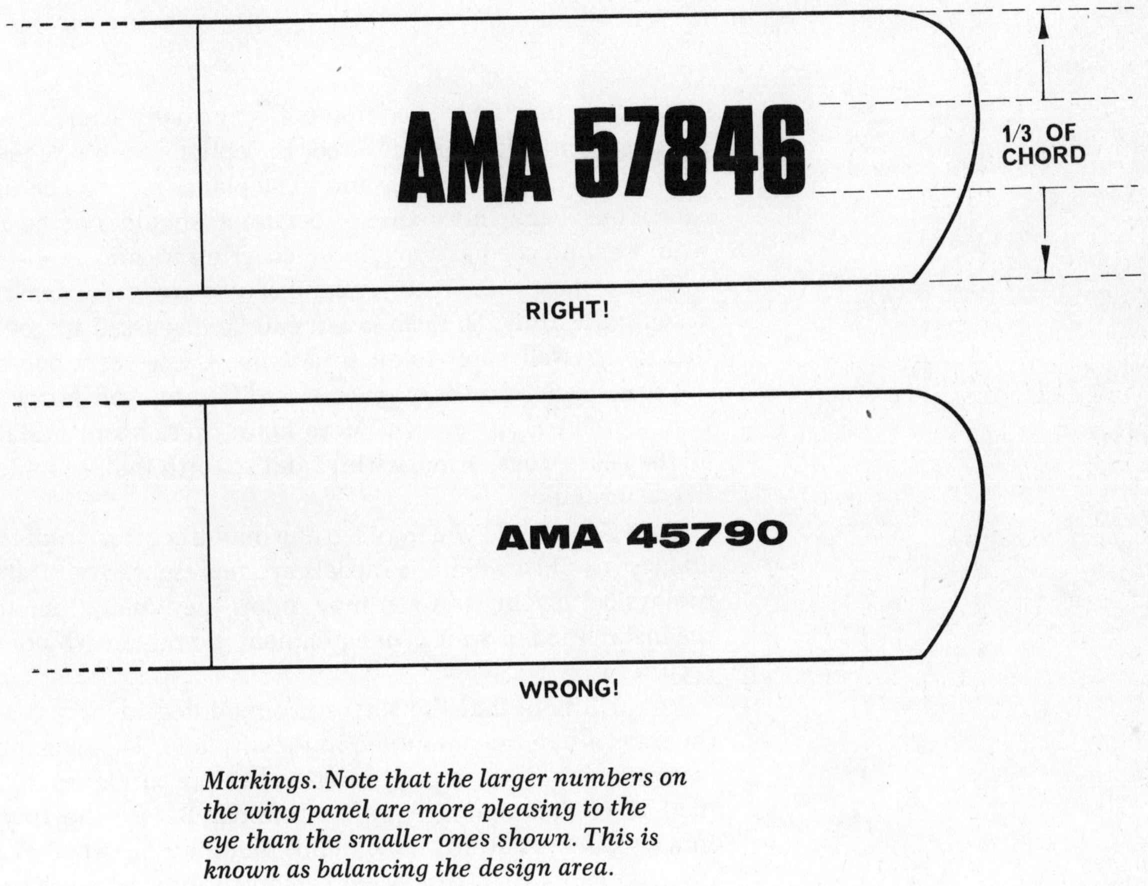

AMA 57846

1/3 OF
CHORD

RIGHT!

AMA 45790

WRONG!

Markings. Note that the larger numbers on the wing panel are more pleasing to the eye than the smaller ones shown. This is known as balancing the design area.

12
Installation of Equipment

The time to install radio equipment is normally after the airframe has been completed and covered. Exceptions to this sequence are in the cases of scale models and some planes having ailerons; both exceptions being ones that a beginner should not be involved with, we'll proceed as though the covering was on.

Today, most radio receivers and servos are of the same general design outwardly, so installation can be discussed in generalities that pretty well apply to all situations. A few years ago this was not true; each and every piece was different, and every installation a problem all its own. More hours were spent fiddling with all the gears, cogs, arms, wiring, and so forth than in building the whole airplane!

Therefore, while you may see one manufacturer's radio receiver and servos illustrated, his models are representative of almost all in physical layout, and you may follow the illustrations to aid in the installation of your own equipment, no matter who the manufacturer may be.

You will note that the servos are mounted in "trays" and that the trays are in turn mounted in the airplane. This is a quick and easy method of putting all in or out of the airplane, and it is a method of dampening engine vibration. Before the trays came into use, servos were individually mounted on wooden rails or plywood decks that were often cemented into the airplane before the servos were installed—a real "Tweedledum and Tweedle-dee" process, with every other screw guaranteed to drop into the

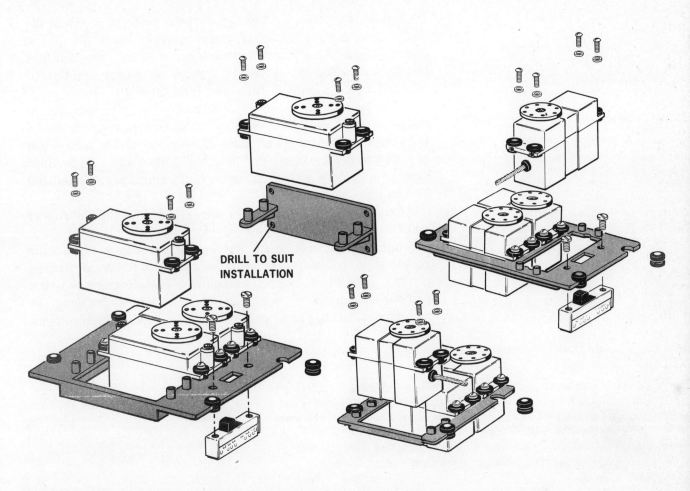

DRILL TO SUIT
INSTALLATION

Manufacturer's servo trays should be used whenever possible in order
to dampen vibration and facilitate servo installation and removal.
A few tray configurations are shown in these sketches.

innards and stubbornly refuse to leave, even with violent shaking.

Today's trays are held in the airframe by usually no more than four screws that pass through rubber grommets inserted in the cutouts along the edge of the tray. The grommets are to dampen vibration between tray and airframe, so when installing the fully assembled tray, do *not* squash the grommets flat when putting in the screws. You want the screws in snugly enough to keep the tray from shifting, but that's as snug as you go!

The same is true of the screws and grommets used to mount the servos to the tray—snug, but no squish!

Installing the servos with the tiny screws can be a hairy experience unless you are blessed with steel nerves and the hands of a midget jeweler. Before you throw the whole set in the ash can, purchase a "screw holder" screwdriver. It has two spring steel jaws that come down past the blade, slip under the head of the screw, and pull it up tight against the blade as it sits in the slot of the screwhead. Even with this marvelous tool, it's wise to do the assembly in a place where you can find the screw if it flips out of the screwdriver. Speckled tile floors, shag rugs, and littered hobby rooms are loads of fun—I've tried them all. . . .

Before installing rails on which to mount the servo tray, bolt in the engine and muffler. (Yes, *muffler*. You are just getting into a hobby that some people find noisy. If too many find it noisy—end of places to fly, or worse—end of hobby. Either way, all your nice new equipment is wasted. So get a muffler and *use it*—and not as a paperweight!)

After your engine and muffler are installed, install the rudder and elevator if you haven't already done so.

Strap the wing in place and put the whole model on a balancing rack that you will stop to make out of a piece of flat wood, such as plywood (roughly 1 foot square and at least ½ inch thick), and two dowels, each a ¼ inch in diameter and 12 inches long. To make the balancing rack, drill two ¼-inch holes at right angles,

Balancing rack. This sketch shows a balancing rack that is quick and easy to construct from scraps. The plane is hung on the rack at a point approximately one-third of the way back from the leading edge of the wing. Plane should hang level, or slightly nose down when viewed from the side, with the rack sitting on a level surface.

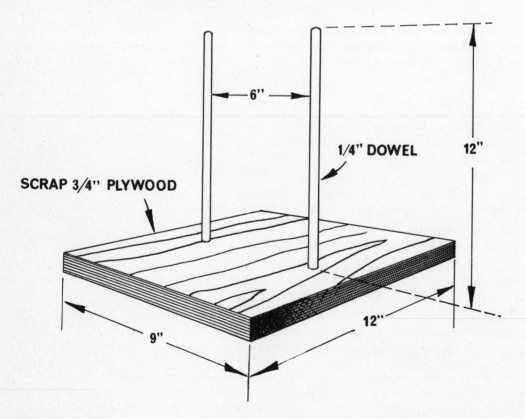

6 inches apart in the flat wood piece, seeing to it that the two holes are somewhat centered in relation to each other and the flat piece of wood. Next, smear one end of each dowel with white glue and push that end into the hole in the flat piece, being sure that each dowel is at right angles to the board. When it all dries, you have a balancing rack—and are ready to put your plane on it.

Place the upright dowels at points on the wing, equidistant from each side of the fuselage, and about a third of the way back from the leading edge of the wing. Assuming that you did all this on a flat table with equal length upright legs, the model should hang in a level attitude with the table—level being the position of wing, fuselage, and elevator as drawn on the plans. If it angles slightly down at the nose, fine. If it is slightly down at the tail, slip the battery pack into the position shown on the plans and see if this corrects the condition. If so, fine; if not, you now need to add weight to the nose. This is done with BBs—adding a few at a time, then epoxying in place, unless the tail hits the table and stays there—in which case you need to visit a plumber's supply shop and buy lead bars. . . .

Assuming that you built reasonably well, and that the model needs but slight weighting on either end, you will need to pick the furthermost forward or rearward point where you can safely deposit and cement BBs and, using a small paper cup balanced on that point, begin adding BBs until the model balances, or hangs slightly nose down.

Why "slightly nose down"? Good question! The reason for this is that an airplane must at all times maintain flying speed, otherwise it stalls and drops to swoop up and enter another stall, and so on, and so on into the ground. While a free-flight model can fly beautifully in a perfectly balanced condition, the R/C model has been found to operate more efficiently with a slightly nose-heavy condition that will allow easier wind penetration—something a model flying by itself is not concerned with.

Once the plane sits on the balancing rack with a *slightly* heavy nose condition, the wing may be removed and the components of the control system laid in place, including the foam wrappings of receiver and battery pack. At this point, let's stop and discuss that foam wrapping. It is lightly mentioned in manufacturers' literature and on plans, but seldom specified as to *what* foam.

Do not use foam rubber! Foam rubber has an inherent energy factor; i.e., force socked into it has almost the same rebound force. Therefore, let's suppose that your model comes into a field at 35 mph—and meets a tree. The model will of course stop quite rapidly—but the battery pack and receiver, wrapped in foam rubber, will continue to go forward to the limit of the material, and then the material will send it backward at the same rate of

Protect all parts with the use of polyurethane foam as shown here to avoid damage to both plane and radio equipment in hard landings.

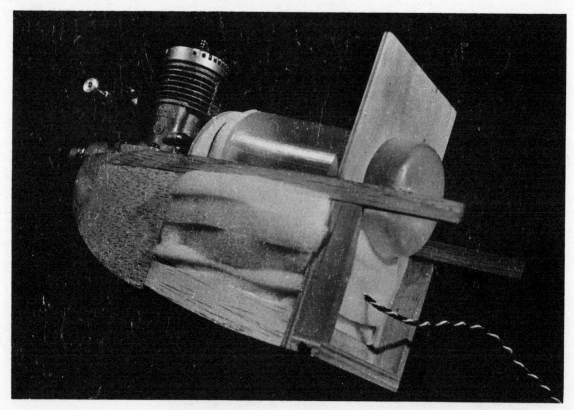

A complete engine installation as it would appear if removed from the plane. Note that the fuel tank is mounted so that its center is in line with carburetor intake and that the battery, the heaviest component of the airborne R/C pack, is packed in foam and placed in a position where it can do no damage in the event of a hard landing.

knots as the initial forward speed of impact. Result: anyone's guess, but it is a known fact that foam rubber in a plane is disastrous at best—like building in a two-way slingshot.

Therefore, the foam to use is the low-reflex polyurethane type one finds used for filter purposes in air conditioners, or the pulpy types of low-grade styrofoam—either one offering good forward impact cushioning with little or no recoil energy.

Now that all the gear is in place and lightly taped with masking tape to prevent shifting, with protective foam included, the wing is placed back on the plane, and the whole works is placed back on the balancing rack. If a big difference shows up, it is now a matter of moving the control components forward or backward to achieve that all-important balance.

Here it is *important* to note that to achieve balance, the battery pack is *never* placed in *any* position other than *closest to the nose of the plane* in relation to the other components! *Never* have it mounted to the rear of the receiver or servos! In event of a crash, this heaviest of all elements will come forward quickly—right through all in its way.

With all the foregoing achieved, we can now get down to

Servo and battery wires should be routed neatly in the fuselage. Study this installation photo carefully for proper equipment layout and installation.

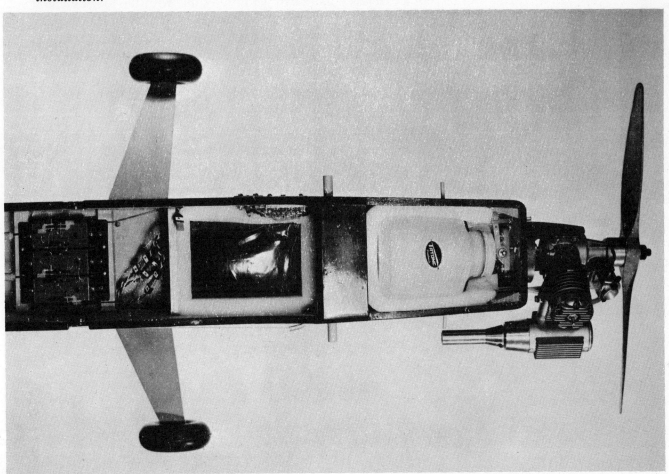

mounting the components in their proper positions, as determined by the balance testing. Servo rails are ready to be glued or epoxied in position and push rods connected to servos. Be sure the rails are parallel to each other so that the tray, when installed, is not forced to twist to conform to the rails.

Once the tray is mounted on the rails, and the receiver and battery pack are in place, it's time to install the final parts of the push rod units, and here we should digress a bit and consider the various push rod installations available. There are the flexible plastic tubes within tubes; stranded cable in plastic tubes; and wire and dowel or square-balsa-type rigid rods that require no guide or support. You should be aware from the outset that the plastic-within-plastic type is subject to heat and cold—stretching in hot weather, shrinking in cold. Many fliers live with the problem by adjusting the linkages to suit the weather, but there are those who claim that this is idiocy—reason being that on a day when the temperature is 90 degrees and the flyer makes the necessary adjustments to bring elevator, rudder, and ailerons back into alignment, he overcomes the temperature of the model in the air as it travels at high speeds and cools itself—only to make the plastic tubing shrink and throw all three control surfaces into another off-true position. While that argument rages, let's look at the next two alternatives.

Stranded metal cable within a plastic tube is not subject to the expansion and contraction of a plastic tube in the same usage, but a careless builder can get into trouble with the metal cable if he forgets one of the cardinal rules of R/C: "No metal-to-metal contact." While the metal cable is perfectly safe sliding back and forth in its plastic tube guide, it can create havoc if it should be in contact with some metal part overlooked by the builder.

Attaching wire to birch dowel push rods.

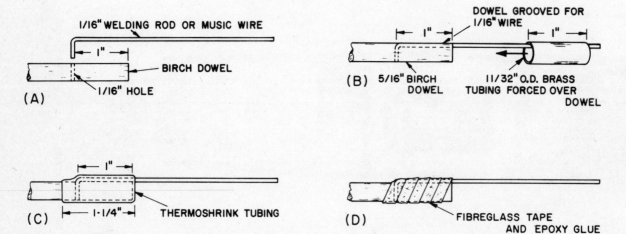

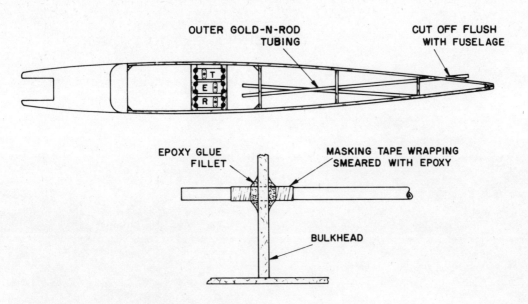

OUTER GOLD-N-ROD TUBING

CUT OFF FLUSH WITH FUSELAGE

EPOXY GLUE FILLET

MASKING TAPE WRAPPING SMEARED WITH EPOXY

BULKHEAD

Installation of hollow tubing to accept flexible push rods.

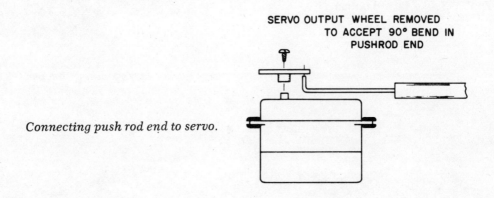

SERVO OUTPUT WHEEL REMOVED TO ACCEPT 90° BEND IN PUSHROD END

Connecting push rod end to servo.

The rigid push rod is more difficult to make and install than the flexible types described above and a bit harder to achieve final small adjustments with, but many fliers still prefer this old standby to achieve less "slop," or play, in the control surfaces, and this takes us back to the actual installation of the push rods—no matter what type you choose to use.

No matter the type chosen, connection between servo and rod, and surface and rod should be as slop-free as possible. A part of this has to do with hinges—you want ones that are free-moving on their axis but without excess free play or wobble. The same is true of the clevis pins, or connectors, used to connect the push rods to the control horns—always see that the pin of the clevis just fits the hole in the horn. It's always better to try oil, before drilling, in mating these two.

VARIOUS MEANS OF ATTACHING THE PUSH ROD END TO THE SERVO.

Du-Bro Solder Link Retainer.

Rocket City's Swing'N-Keeper.

Du-Bro Kwik-Keeper.

Du-Bro E-Z Connector Control Rod Adapter.

Goldberg Snap'R-Keeper.

Midwest Products nylon push rod retainer.

Why all the fuss about no slop? Picture your model in the air —a 50-mile-an-hour breeze is blowing over surfaces that are free to move up and down a distance of ⅛ inch in either direction. A "flutter" is set up, and the surfaces start a rapid up-and-down dance that can rip them out of their hinges or, worse, beat an expensive servo to death. Or, your plane is in a power dive and needs all the up you can give it to get back to level flight—but sloppy hinges and push rod connections only allow half the needed control surface "throw," especially under the pressures the model is now going through. May as well put down the transmitter and look for a shovel.

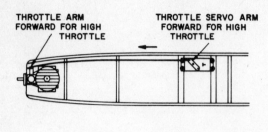

THROTTLE ARM
FORWARD FOR HIGH
THROTTLE

THROTTLE SERVO ARM
FORWARD FOR HIGH
THROTTLE

MODE II TRANSMITTER
SHOWN - STICKS REVERSED
ON MODE I

HIGH
THROTTLE

Throttle servo location.

HIGH
T

*Identifying the throttle servo
function, mode, and direction of
travel.*

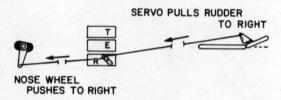

SERVO PULLS RUDDER
TO RIGHT

T
E
R

NOSE WHEEL
PUSHES TO RIGHT

*Make certain rudder/nosegear
servo operates both controls
properly.*

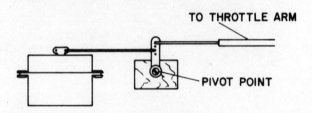

TO THROTTLE ARM

PIVOT POINT

*One arm of an aileron bellcrank
mounted on a plywood base and
epoxied to the fuselage side can be
used to increase or decrease the
throw of a linear output servo to
match the throttle arm movement
of your engine.*

Whether using plastic, or stranded metal cable within plastic, either should be well supported within its housing for as long a distance as possible before making its exit and final connection. If left unguided, either will buckle under air pressure loads and render the servo's effort almost useless. With plastic tubing as the drive rod, use wire, normally $\frac{1}{16}$ inch, as the final part of the rod, with no more than an inch of the slave plastic tube protruding from the larger guide tubing on either end.

With the stranded metal cable, allow only an inch to protrude from each end of the guide tubing, then use a short length of brass tubing to couple the cable and the right length of threaded steel rod that will connect into the clevis pin. (If you happen to have an acquaintance who strums a guitar, his old base strings are excellent stranded metal cables.

Before hooking push rods to servos, check to see that you have the right servo in the right place and that it will match its push rod and control function. (Even experienced flyers often goof on this one!) This is done by switching on the receiver and the transmitter and sending some commands, making note of which servo moves to what command. Label each servo as to its job, for example, "Rudder," "Elevator," "Motor." If you have them mounted in the wrong places, simply unplug them from the receiver and replug them into their proper places to perform as required.

While it is not mandatory, try to use the outside connection of the wheel or arm of the servo as it sits in the tray with the others. This is to be sure that your push rods will not be in each other's way as they go to work.

With control horns installed on surfaces as shown on the plans and hinges installed as per manufacturer's instructions, elevator and rudder are taped in position with strips of masking tape applied on both sides to hold them firmly in place. The inner rod of the push rod system is now inserted into the larger guide rod, with a length of threaded-end rod epoxied into one end of the inner rod and an unthreaded piece into the other end. The threaded end is fitted with a clevis pin and the clevis is attached to the proper control horn.

Since the average control horn has from three to four holes, you will no doubt wonder which hole to use for the clevis pin. Use the outer hole, or one farthest from the control surface. This

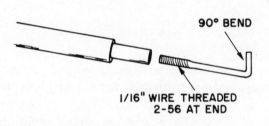

Clevis connection for Gold-N-Rod.

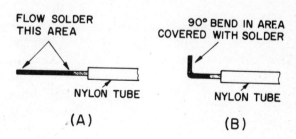

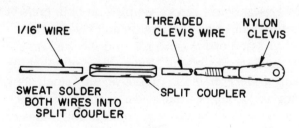

Servo connection for stranded cable.

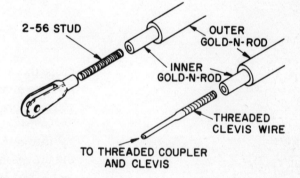

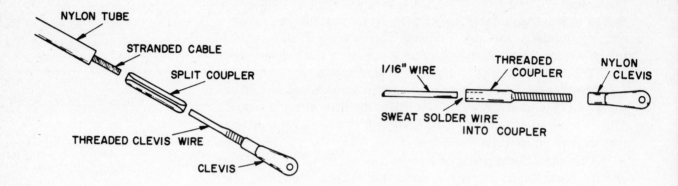

Clevis connection for stranded cable.

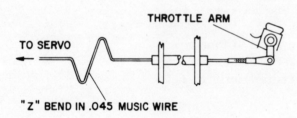

A simple throttle override device.

gives the least amount of movement or "throw," to the surface, thereby giving less abrupt control in flight—the safest route for you as a beginner.

Moving to the inside of the fuselage, and the servos, bend an "L" into one end of a length of $\frac{1}{16}$-inch wire and insert this from the underside into the proper side of the wheel or arm of the correct servo for the rod just fitted, using the outside hole on the wheel or arm. On the end protruding upward, install a "wheel collar." This collar will hold the wire in place and allow for easy removal if the need arises. *Never* put clevis pins on both ends of a push rod. Vibration will unscrew them quite quickly!

Next, line up the wire end of the push rod and the wire on the servo. Cut the two so they are about $\frac{1}{8}$ inch shy of touching each other; then slip a piece of brass tubing about 1 inch long over the wires to act as a coupler, and solder it in place. When doing this soldering, be sure to use a heat sink on both sides of the joint to avoid burning up the servo wheel or arm on one end, and the plastic drive rod on the other. Proceed to next installation and repeat the process. Before checking to see how the installed rods work, remember to remove the masking tape that's holding the surfaces in position!

With the push rod units hooked up, find a quiet corner, turn off the radio and television and get rid of anyone present. Turn on the transmitter and send some signals to each servo in turn. Hold the control stick at its extreme limit, for, say, rudder; then place your ear next to the fuselage and listen carefully. If you hear nothing, fine. If you hear a faint groaning noise, you have the control linkage too long or too short. The servo is dutifully trying to do its job for you, but if you don't correct the linkage, the servo will burn itself out in fairly short order.

In some instances you will find it difficult to install a linkage and not have the servo moan at either end of its limits. These will most often occur with the throttle linkages to the engine because this unit has a definite set of limitations on the distance it can travel in either direction. Here, we fudge a bit, and install an override device to keep the servo happy. This device can be one purchased over the counter or one you make yourself. To make it yourself, you need to remember the basic problem of override: The servo wishes to travel its full length, while the part to be moved has a limit to which it will move. To overcome this, you need to build in a "cushion," or safety release. This may be done by placing a V bend in the final wire-connecting rod, so that the open V absorbs the extra energy of the servo's push.

Further cushioning effect is obtained by bending an N shape into the rod, and is recommended if there is doubt that a V offers enough override spacing for the servo. You may next try a W, but it's better to do a little investigation to see *why* the servo is overriding in the first place. Chances are that the wire rod is too long or too short.

Installation of the switch for the power pack in the plane can be done in several ways, but no matter which manner you choose, try to make it as idiot-proof as possible so that you always know which switch position is "on," and which is "off," and never be afraid to label it.

Many fliers mount the switch on the exterior of the fuselage so it operates in a line with the plane's flight path. To them, forward is "ON," and as though stopping the flight, pushing to the rear is "OFF." Others mount the switch vertically, with the up position being "ON," and the down, or earth, side being "OFF." Still others prefer the switch inside the airplane with a wire push rod to the exterior. With this system, pulling the rod out turns the set on, pushing in turns it off. This is done for two reasons: to keep fuel and dirt out of the switch by placing it inside the plane, and to avoid the set being accidently turned on, thus draining the bat-

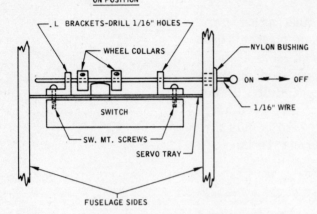

CROSS SECTION VIEW
ON POSITION

L BRACKETS-DRILL 1/16" HOLES
WHEEL COLLARS
NYLON BUSHING
ON → OFF
1/16" WIRE
SWITCH
SW. MT. SCREWS
SERVO TRAY
FUSELAGE SIDES

Simple method of mounting a switch inside the fuselage without drilling the switch button.

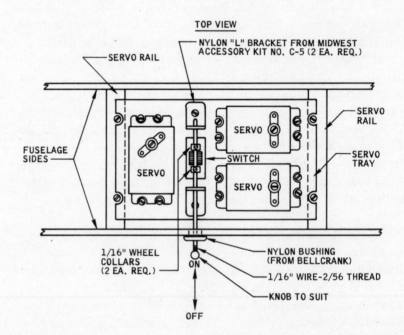

TOP VIEW

NYLON "L" BRACKET FROM MIDWEST
ACCESSORY KIT NO. C-5 (2 EA. REQ.)
SERVO RAIL
SERVO
SERVO RAIL
FUSELAGE SIDES
SWITCH
SERVO
SERVO TRAY
SERVO
1/16" WHEEL COLLARS (2 EA. REQ.)
NYLON BUSHING (FROM BELLCRANK)
ON
1/16" WIRE-2/56 THREAD
KNOB TO SUIT
OFF

teries, as the wire rod could hardly ever be accidently *pulled* into the "ON" position.

To place the switch inside the plane, see the method illustrated in the sketches.

Of next concern is the placement of the antenna. Before you decide the antenna is too long to fit neatly between here and there, put down the snippers and make arrangements to leave it *as is!* The antenna is a carefully measured length for a reason, all to do with maximum reception. Aside from esthetics, if a bit of it is left to flutter in the breeze, let it!

As important as an antenna's length is the business of getting it immediately out of the fuselage in as short a distance as possible from the receiver. DON'T lead it in or around the servos! Servos set up false signals to the receiver when placed close to the antenna. Be sure to tie a knot in the antenna before the point where it exits the fuselage, or put a restrainer on it so that no strain is placed on the point where it is attached to the receiver.

Safety plate to avoid pulling the antenna loose from the receiver can be made from scrap, plywood or plastic.

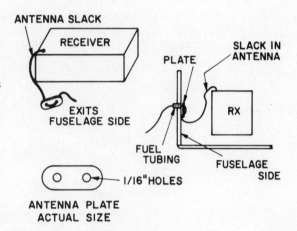

The end of the antenna may be fastened to either rudder or elevator tip with the aid of a small rubber band knotted around the antenna, then stretched and hooked over a pin imbedded in one of the two surfaces. If you're the type who cares, you can use a glass bead type of pin and choose a pin of the color that matches your plane.

Equally important is the business of getting all servo and battery pack wires into neat order. All should be coursed away from the servos and away from the receiver. While this may seem an impossibility, it *can* be done. Loop them away from servos and receiver, and bury them under the foam packing used to protect the working units. This is to stop electronic noise within the plane and also to keep the wiring away from abrasion or interference with servo wheels or push rod units.

Now that all this is installed and ready to go, there is one more point to make note of and remember at all times—batteries. If yours are of the nickel cadmium ("nicad") type, you *must* remember to charge them at regular intervals during the flying season, *and* during the winter months when the batteries are not in use. More about this in the section devoted to maintenance.

Almost the same care must be exercised with the units using standard alkaline or mercury-type batteries. These must be watched very carefully and a log kept of the time of actual usage. Whether flown or not, the latter type of batteries should be thrown out after three months and new ones purchased when one is ready to fly again. *Never* leave them in a plane or transmitter for long periods, such as over the winter. To do so will usually result in acidic damage to contacts and wiring should a battery swell and burst.

13
Engine
Maintenance

During the building of your plane, be sure that your new engine is not sitting out, catching all the balsa dust and other stray dirt that may be around. The same is true once the plane is finished and the engine is installed in the nose, whether the plane is at home or at the flying field. Any dirt in the precisely fitted innards, with the engine turning up to 12,000 and more revolutions a minute, and you can well imagine the grinding process that would take place!

Your first step in proper maintenance is a careful breaking-in of the engine. This is done on a test stand, and *never* in the plane itself. (This is to avoid needless wear and tear on the motor mounts and radio gear due to possible backfiring, rough running, and the like.) Although you may buy a ready-made one, a test stand can be any piece of plywood cut to accept the engine, and large enough to be clamped to a supporting unit, such as a saw horse, porch railing, old table, and so forth. Holes are drilled in the plywood to accept bolts passed through the holes in the mounting lugs of the engine, and the engine is bolted securely to the stand, with emphasis on "securely." Next, two screw hooks are driven in, about 4 or 5 inches apart, in a parallel line with the rear of the engine, to act as anchors for rubber bands laced from one to the other over your fuel tank.

A word about fuel tank locations. For a reason best known to nature, deep thinkers, and engine designers, a fuel tank must always be mounted in a plane, or on a test stand, with the fuel

Engine Test Stand. The entire unit is fully adjustable to suit any engine. The wing nuts to the right and left of the engine hold down blocks, which in turn, clamp over the engine's mounting lugs. The fuel tank, blocked up so that the outlet is horizontal with the fuel inlet of the engine, is held in place here with rubber bands. Test stand is held to bench or other firm surface by "C" clamps.

line exit at the same, or near same, level as the fuel connection of the engine, when both are viewed from the side. The tank is also mounted as near the engine as possible, within the bounds of common sense of course, being sure that it isn't so close as to burn the end of the tank with the heat of the engine. The other extreme was tried by a modeler I once helped get started—he proudly brought his first plane to my house for a check-out. Among other massive boo-boos, this fellow had his fuel tank mounted neatly—between receiver and servos, ready and willing to slop fuel all over the vital electronic works and render them instantly useless beyond any doubt on the first flight—if the plane was even able to get airborne!

Follow the manufacturer's instructions for starting, and by all means make it a point to read the *entire* manufacturer's information sheet that comes with the engine. Too many ignore these informative words and then wonder why their engines perform poorly. Also be sure to do your engine running outside (even these little fellows put out deadly carbon monoxide!) in a dirt-free area.

Various manufacturers specify different lengths of time for the break-in period, but most fall between 45 minutes and an hour. This means total time, not time for one long, constant run. New engines should be run for no more than 10 minutes the first time, and then no more than 20 minutes in each subsequent running, always allowing the engine to cool completely before starting the next break in session. Also be sure that you run the engine "rich" during the break in time, and avoid the urge to hear the mighty scream of power by thinning out the mixture. (On a rich setting the engine should sound "soupy.")

After each running, whether breaking in or actual flight usage, wipe the engine clean with a lint-free rag, and drape the rag over it to keep out dirt. The fuel contains a goodly amount of lubricant, and if left on an engine it will cook onto the metal and be far more difficult to remove than grease burned onto a frying pan. Aside from an ugly appearance, an engine with burned-on lubricant cannot cool properly because this gunk is stopping the cooling fins from doing their job. This will result in loss of power and in accelerated wear.

If you are clever enough to read the engine manufacturer's directions thoroughly, you will find suggested propeller sizes listed on most information sheets. Select the one that shows the lower RPMs on the chart and use this for the break-in. If the manufacturer shows no recommended propeller sizes other than a general size, see the chart at the end of this chapter, and choose the lowest pitch prop shown for your size engine.

Also when purchasing props, keep a very practical verse in mind:

> For engines up to .29,
> Nylon props are mighty fine.
> For .35, and larger size,
> Nylon props are plain unwise!

This bit of knock-kneed verse is one to be remembered in prop selection. Nylon props are great for the beginner because they do not break when the plane comes in for a nose-first landing, while the other available type, wood, is almost guaranteed to break every time. BUT, *on an engine over .29 size, a nylon prop can be a potential killer. It can disintegrate under the high RPM forces and cause disastrous results. Flyers have had these disintegrated blades imbed themselves in arms, chests, and, worse, eyes. Even on the size engines where nylon props are allowable, the props should be boiled for a minimum of a half-hour, then left in the boiling water to cool along with the water. This somehow relieves the molding tensions of the nylon and makes the prop safe, but this method does not work on props for the larger-size engines.* For .35's and larger, use wood props!

Any prop, nylon or wood, should be balanced before bolting it onto the engine. A nylon prop, due to its having been made in a master mold, will be quite close to equilibirium and can be made to balance perfectly by scraping the back side of the prop with the flat side of a single-edge razor blade out toward the tip of the prop. Wood props can also be similarly balanced by scraping with a razor blade, or if *way* out of balance, by using a sandpaper pad, again, on the *back* of the heavy side. To achieve initial balance, put a 3- or 4-inch dowel, of the same size as the prop hole, into the prop hole with an equal amount projecting on each side of the prop. Next, open the jaws of a vise about 2 inches and place the dowel across the opening so that the prop is parallel to the opening of the jaws, being sure that the vise is on a level surface. You can soon determine if the prop is in balance or not and make the needed corrections. This balancing is highly important with an R/C model because of—you guessed it—vibration! The pounding of a single-cylinder engine sets up throb enough, but when it is compounded by a prop even slightly out of balance, the effect on a radio and other components is disastrous!

Vibration can also loosen mounting bolts, so be sure to check these during the break-in period and particularly after installation of the engine in the plane. Be sure to use lock washers under the head of each mounting bolt. In mounting the engine in your plane, you can take a measure to help dampen some of the vibration by placing rubber grommets on each bolt between motor mount and engine mounting lug, and between lock washer and mounting lug; or using a strip of foam rubber, the length of the mounting lug, cemented to the motor mounts at the place where the engine sits, with another strip cemented to the top of the mounting lugs.

In the break-in period, a new engine will often stop for no apparent reason and refuse to start until it cools off. This is to be expected and should cause no concern on your part. Just a case of new metals getting used to working together by adjusting to each other's temperament. Once an engine is broken in though, this sort of behavior is unacceptable and there is usually a good reason that can be traced back to negligence on your part.

If a broken-in engine refuses to start at all, check the obvious parts, beginning with the glow plug and starting battery. An easy method of doing this is to take the plug out of the engine and connect it to the battery. If the wire coil in the plug glows a bright orange, the trouble lies elsewhere, but if there is no glow, either the plug is deficient or the battery is dead. If a fresh plug also fails to glow, the battery is of course no good and the problem is solved. However, it may not be dead at all; so don't be hasty in throwing it away. With current as low as 1½ volts, oil on the battery clip that attaches to the glow plug can effectively insulate the clip and stop the current from reaching the coil. Always keep the clip and the plug clean, and, too, be sure that the battery terminals and the wires to them are clean and making good contact.

If battery and plug test out OK, the next point to check is the opening in the carburetor, particularly if you fly from a dirt or grass field. Dirt would obviously block off fuel flow, and although grass is considered "clean," its seeds, clippings, and the varmints that live in it are all troublemakers in a carburetor. Since you will need to prime your engine to start it, get a small plastic bottle with a spout that allows a fine stream of fuel to come out when the bottle is squeezed. This same "priming bottle" can be used to flush out the carburetor by firing a burst of fuel into the opening, then turning the plane upside down and cranking the prop around several times to get the excess fuel and dirt out. Be sure the battery clip is not connected when you do this!

If the engine still refuses to start, check the screws that hold the head on the cylinder. If they are loose, there'll be no compression and no starts. Use care in tightening the screws so that you don't damage the head slots.

Next, examine your fuel tank and fuel line for dirt and for tightness of fuel line fit to both tank and engine. A leak at either fitting or a hole in the fuel line will result in little or no fuel reaching the engine.

Have you kept your fuel tightly capped? If not, go get a new can of fuel. The volatile parts of fuel are methyl alcohol and nitromethane, both fast evaporators. If you leave fuel cans open, or store fuel for long periods, the main ingredient left in the can is lubricant, and although the engine needs it desperately, it won't run on it alone.

Another word about fuels: when buying your first fuel, buy only a small can at a time, and do not buy the high-nitro type for the break-in period, or for three or four hours' running after initial break-in. High nitro has less lubricant and can damage a new engine where lubrication is very important. After the engine is well broken in you can use a high-nitro fuel, but this will depend mainly on the area in which you live, and on climatic variation. It is vital to remember that the fuel you fly with on one day may simply not get you in the air on another. This is due to temperature and humidity conditions, and flyers unaware of the effects that weather changes have on an engine have bought new engines after trying to get airborne on a hot, humid day with no luck. This is particularly true along the eastern seaboard of the United States, where temperature and humidity can each equal 96 on a summer's day. On days like this, only high-nitro fuel will perform in an engine.

This is called "heat sag," and it affects more than just the engine. As the temperature goes up, efficiency of lifting surfaces, wing and tail, go down. This, coupled with a sluggish engine, often keeps a plane grounded that performs beautifully on cooler, drier days. There are also days that are deceptive, such as a rainy day that seems reasonably cool (remember, modelers fly in *any* weather). The high humidity on such a day keeps a lot of otherwise adequately powered planes grounded. Experimentation with fuels of varying nitro content is the only answer to your particular problem in your particular location.

Glow plugs, like fuels, can affect engine performance under varying climactic conditions. On one day, a "hot" plug works best with a certain fuel, while on the next day, a cool plug is the only answer. So—have a couple of each in your field box, as well as two or three small cans of fuel, each with varying degrees of nitro content.

The same is true of props. Have a selection of diameter and pitch sizes in your field box at all times. There is no such thing as one perfect prop for all occasions, and don't let anyone convince you otherwise! There are times when you will want the "bite" of an 8-inch pitch, and times when you will need the smoothness of a 3- or 4-inch pitch. It's all up to Mother Nature—and your judgment.

How does one know for certain that he has the right plug, the right fuel, and the right prop for any given day? If you're halfway thorough, the solution is simple—make a record in a small notebook by noting the temperature and humidity on a series of days as reported by the radio or TV weather programs for your *specific area:* i.e., low humidity, low temperature-medium humidity, medium temperature, and similar facts. Then, with the aid of a pull scale such as used to weigh fish, test various combinations of props, fuels, and plugs (the "PFP test") to see which gives the greatest amount of pull on the scale when it is attached between the tail wheel of your plane and an immovable object with the engine running full out. (If you have no fish-weighing scale, use two or three No. 64 rubber bands between the tail and the stationary object, and mark the distance the plane travels on the ground with each PFP test.) The greatest pull, or distance obtained, is of course made with the best combination of PFP and should be noted as the one to use on similar days.

An engine should be periodically removed from the plane and given a good cleaning with frying pan cleaner. Be careful not to get the cleaner inside the engine. No matter how careful you are, some lubricant will become baked on and should be removed. All screws should be checked for snugness and replaced if ragged around the screw slots. A new fuel line should be installed and the tank removed from the plane and thoroughly cleaned with alcohol. The engine and tank areas should be flushed with alcohol, wiped dry with clean rags or paper towels, and packed with garage floor cleaner or Borax. The packing is removed after 24 hours and the area again cleaned with alcohol to remove the last residue of the packing. This packing method is to remove fuel that has seeped into cracks and crevices, and although the term "packing" is used, it need not be taken literally. A ¼-inch layer of cleaner on all areas constantly exposed to fuel is sufficient. If you did a good job of coating the engine and tank areas with epoxy or fiberglass resin, chances are that alcohol is all that's needed for a good cleanup.

Checklist.

Here are some worthwhile precautions to take:

1. Following each flight, cover the engine with a clean cloth after carefully wiping away all the collected oil residue from engine and surrounding areas.

2. Upon returning home from the flying field, use a toothbrush to clean all exterior parts of the engine and surrounding areas with rubbing alcohol or lighter fluid. (A search through a supermarket will reveal some cheap buys on either.)

3. If you see obvious dirt around an engine opening (intake or exhaust), remove it before dousing the engine with the cleaning fluids mentioned.

4. If you're flying weekly, remove the engine from the plane once a month and soak it in rubbing alcohol to remove built-up fuel residues. At yearly intervals use a product such as Sunbeam Metal Clean (directions on container) to thoroughly clean off cooked-on grease.

5. After weekly or yearly cleanings, put a few drops of sewing machine oil in the carburetor intake and the exhaust port, rotate the engine about 10 times, and cover the engine with a clean cloth held in place by rubber bands. Do NOT use plastic bags to cover an engine. Plastic causes condensation with temperature changes and can possibly lead to rust or, worse, acid build-up in an engine.

6. After each flying session, drain the fuel tank and clean it by flushing rubbing alcohol through until it is thoroughly clean. Fuel is a combination of ultra-fast- and ultra-slow-drying ingredients. To leave them sitting in a tank will only result in a stubborn sludge that will clog fuel lines and filters.

Prop Chart

RADIO CONTROL

Engine Size	Pattern Sport	Scale	Pylon Racing	Stunt Sport & Scale
.049	6-3, 6-4*	6-4, 7-3		6-3, 6-4
.09	7-3, 7-4	7-4, 8-4		7-4, 7-6
.15	8-4, 8-6, 9-4	8-4, 8-6, 9-4	7-5, 7-6	8-4, 8-5
.19	9-4, 9-5	9-5		9-4, 9-5, 9-6
.23	9-4, 9-5	9-5		9-4, 9-5, 9-6
.29	10-6, 10-9	10-6, 10-9	8-8, 8-8½, 8-9	10-6
.35	10-6	10-6, 11-4		10-6
.40	10-6, 11-4	11-4, 12-4	9-7, 9-8, 9-8½	
.45	11-4, 11-6	12-4, 12-6		11-6
.50	11-6	12-4, 12-6		
.55	11-6, 11-7	12-6, 13-5½		
.60	11-7, 11-7½, 11-8	12-6, 13-5½, 14-4		11-6, 12-6
.70		12-6, 14-4, 14-6		
.80		12-6, 14-4, 14-6		

Courtesy, *Top Flite Models*

* First number shown is *diameter;* second number, after hyphen, is *pitch.*)

14
Preflight
Check-Out

The pilot of an airplane, be it the smallest light plane or a Boeing 747, runs through a preflight check-out to insure that nothing is overlooked on the ground that could cause trouble in the air. The same is true of the R/C flyer; the successful ones check and double-check before and after starting their engines, while the ones who give up the hobby after a string of failures are those who never bother with check-outs.

The check-out is particularly important for the beginner on his first flight, but the procedure is, in part, basically the same one as followed by champions. So before going to the flying field, be sure to do all of the following:

Switch on the transmitter, *then* the receiver, and make it a rule to always follow this same sequence (more about this later). Place your plane on the floor and stand behind it. Look at the antenna on the plane. Is it neatly strung back to the rudder or elevator, or coiled inside the plane? Have you pulled the transmitter antenna out to its fullest length, or is it in the collapsed position? This entire antenna procedure applies to preflight methods at the field too, so you are really practicing now for your first flights, as well as checking out equipment.

As you stand behind the plane, move the stick that controls the rudder to the right. Does the rudder swing to the right, or to the left? If it goes left, you have crossed controls, so move the push rod connection at the servo to the opposite side of the arm or wheel on the servo. If you are using the elevator, move the elevator stick directly forward *away* from you. Does the back edge of the elevator move down toward the floor, or up toward the ceiling? If it moves toward the ceiling, you have another crossed control; correct it.

Move the motor control forward, away from you. Walk over and look into the carburetor opening. Is the hole open, or closed? If closed, you have controls reversed; correct at the servo. Leaving this control reversed, although it might not seem to matter, is bad practice, especially if you have someone help you learn to fly. They will expect the motor control to work like all other motor controls, and this can be important in a panic situation.

Next, check all linkages again to see if any are loose or not properly seated in control horn or servo fitting. Check hinges too for "slop" or play. A *very* small amount of movement is over $\frac{1}{16}$ inch in either direction; determine what causes the problem and correct it. Slightly oversize holes in control horns or servo fittings can cause this unwanted play, and it's for this reason that holes in either horns or fittings should never be enlarged. Instead, use the correct size clevis or wire to fit the existing holes.

Inspect the fuel system to be sure that connections of the fuel line are snug, that there are no bends or kinks in the line, and that nothing is obstructing the breather tube on the fuel tank. Be sure too that the weighted tubing (klunk) inside the tank is long enough to reach the rear of the tank but not so long as to cause it to stick at any one point. It must be free to swing from side to side.

Roll the model on the floor by giving a push and letting it travel free. Does it track straight, or swerve to the right or left? If it does not track straight, stand over the model and check to see if the wheels are parallel to the fuselage sides and, if they are not, bend them until they are. If the wheels *are* parallel, check the tail wheel and correct it until the plane tracks straight. Along with all wheels being parallel, the two main wheels should have a slight amount of camber in them, meaning that when viewed from the front of the plane, the wheels should be closer together at the bottom than at the top. This makes for smoother landings and better tracking.

At this point, type or neatly letter a label with your name, address, and telephone number and the amount of reward, if any, you would pay to get your creation back if lost, and glue it inside the plane.

Standing directly over the plane, do you see that all surfaces are properly lined up? Is the wing at right angles to the fuselage? Is the horizontal stabilizer? Is the rudder lined up with the center line of the fuselage? Hopefully you took care of all this alignment in the earlier building stages, but strange things do happen, and this is the time to catch them. With wing and horizontal stabilizer normally held in place by rubber bands on the simpler planes (the kind *you* started with, we hope), the positioning corrections are easy; but if the rudder is out of line, cut it off and reglue it! A word here about rubber bands used to hold the wing and horizontal stabilizer in place. Use *gum* bands only, and buy them by the box at a stationery store that hopefully sells a lot of them so you are assured of getting fresh ones. The gum bands have more snap than their cheaper cousins, and at least one brand, Arco, is available in almost every city, and town in the country. You will want No. 64 size for holding the wing, and if the horizontal stabilizer isn't glued to the fuselage, you will probably want No. 32 size to hold it to the anchor dowels.

In putting these gum bands on the plane, always X them over the surface to be held in place; i.e., holding the wing on the fuselage with one hand, hook a band over the front left dowel, pull it back, and hook the other end over the rear right dowel. The next band is from front right to the rear left, and this alternating continues until you have enough bands over the wing to allow no movement of the wing when it is pushed, pulled, and tugged at. You must remember that when the plane comes out of a dive, the wing will want to lift greatly due to its fast air speed, while the fuselage with no lift, only weight, will be trying to make the quickest and shortest route to earth. Those bands have to hold!

Once all surfaces are attached, they should be viewed from both front and rear for proper alignment with each other and the fuselage. A wing or horizontal stabilizer tilted up or down on one side will cause the plane to make unwanted turns. This condition is corrected with temporary shims of balsa of the proper thickness. Once the surface is trued up by shimming, a permanent piece is cut and glued to the fuselage in place of the shims.

Balance should be checked once again to be sure that the plane is still in proper trim.

Thrust settings should be checked too in the initial check-out of a model. Going back to the plans, find the thrust line as indicated on the side view of the fuselage. If no thrust line is shown, draw a line through the exact center of the drawing of the engine, being sure that your line is parallel to the crankshaft lines indicated. Do the same on the top view of the plane. These are the thrust lines.

Next, draw a line at right angles to the thrust line in the exact center of the space indicated for a propeller on the engine drawing. If you are using a 10-inch prop on your plane, extend this new line for 5 inches on each side of the thrust center line and make a mark at the end of the 5 inches. Do the same on the top view of the engine. This represents the angle line of your prop as installed on your plane.

A line is now drawn from the upper prop tip point on the side view to an obvious point on the fuselage such as the point where the leading edge of the wing rests. Next draw a line from the lower prop tip point to a point on the bottom of the fuselage, such as the place where the landing gear is attached. Using pieces of thread the same lengths as these two new lines, check the distances on your plane to determine if you are reasonably close to the down thrust settings indicated on the plans. Correct with washers between engine and bearers if needed.

To check side thrust, draw lines from your indicated prop tip points back to equal positions on each horizontal stabilizer, determined by measuring out an exact number of inches from the center line of the stab on both sides. Transfer the stab measurements to your plane, and again use lengths of thread to check for reasonable accuracy in the side thrust setting. Loosen bolts and twist engine to a new setting if required.

Give your plane a gentle shake. Does anything clunk or rattle? The only one allowed is in the so-called "clunk" type of fuel tank, and the noise you might get from wheels as they move back and forth on the axles. Anything else is a no-no; so if you have noises, look in the fuselage and check for a loose receiver or battery pack and repack the culprit in foam. It often happens that an originally neat installation becomes a bit messy as a plane works its way toward final assembly, the receiver and batteries being constantly shifted as servo connections and other details are finalized. Even if no rattle is heard, give the innards a complete check to be sure that all is well padded and firmly in place and that no wiring is in a position to be rubbed by moving parts or so loose as to be able to get in a position to be rubbed by, or interfere with, servo action.

Take the antenna off the transmitter. On most, this is simply a case of unscrewing the antenna as though it itself were a large screw. (If the antenna does not unscrew easily, check the manufacturer's literature to be sure about method of attachment before applying a wrench and demolishing the whole works.) Switch on the transmitter after the antenna is removed and then switch on the power in the plane. Walk slowly back from the plane, giving a rudder right signal with each step backward. You should be able to reach a distance of roughly 20 feet from the plane before the rudder quits responding to your commands. If you are only able to get 10 feet or less of range, send receiver and transmitter back to the manufacturer and let *them* solve the problem. Don't fly it!

15
Building a Field Box*

Peace of mind on the flying field contributes greatly to flying ability. If all your equipment is working perfectly, most of your worries can be left at work, or at home, and all you have to do is fly, fly, fly!

The One Tripper, if properly built, was designed to operate completely problem-free. It is so convenient that you barely notice it beside you, ready to do what you ask it, without demanding a thing from you except knowledge on how to operate it and a little respect for its components.

The reason it's called the One Tripper is because, with it in one hand and your plane in the other, you can walk from your car to the flight line without having to make one or two more trips for things such as beer, blondes, or screwdrivers. I've always said that one good field box at the flight line is worth two shopping bags in the car.

Here's to trouble-and-worry-free flying and only one trip to the car . . .

Construction

(1) Cut out the box parts from ⅜″ plywood. (For best results use a bench saw with a plywood blade.) Assemble entire box with ¾″ finishing nails, first by nailing sides to ends, and bottom to

---

* Reprint from *R/C Modeler Magazine.*

RCM "One Tripper" field box. A compact unit that carries all the required equipment to the field with you. Full construction details are given in this chapter.

sides and end. Position the divider into the box and secure with nails.

(2) Use screws to secure the wood blocks to the underside of the box. Reinforce the box with wood screws as follows: Drill holes for the screws, ream out to countersink the screw heads and then fit the screws. Use wood filler to cover the screw heads, nails, and any wood blemishes. Allow to dry, and sand the box with fine sandpaper. If you wish, the box can be stained to contrast the wood grain. Brush or spray the box with *polyurethane* varnish [fuelproof!].

(3) Next, cut and shape a piece of strapping to hold the fuel bottle to the box. Use the fuel bottle end plate to support the strapping and fasten to the box with nuts, washers, and bolts. Repeat the above assembly for the transmitter bracket. (Note: The hump in the transmitter bracket is to allow you to turn your transmitter on and off without having to remove it.)

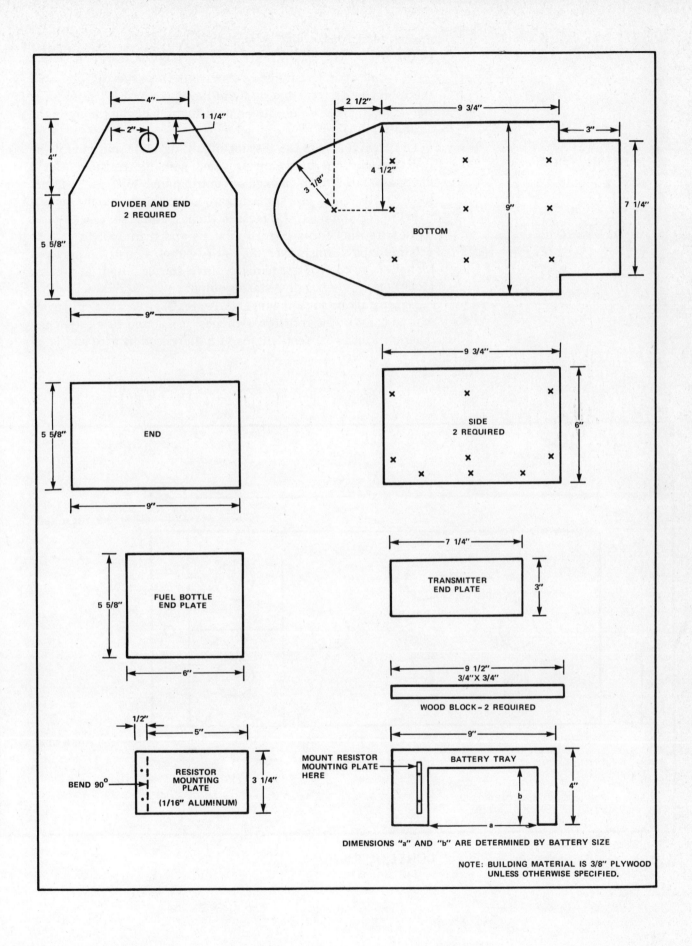

DIVIDER AND END
2 REQUIRED

BOTTOM

END

SIDE
2 REQUIRED

FUEL BOTTLE
END PLATE

TRANSMITTER
END PLATE

WOOD BLOCK – 2 REQUIRED
3/4" X 3/4"

BEND 90°

RESISTOR
MOUNTING
PLATE

(1/16" ALUMINUM)

MOUNT RESISTOR
MOUNTING PLATE
HERE

BATTERY TRAY

DIMENSIONS "a" AND "b" ARE DETERMINED BY BATTERY SIZE

NOTE: BUILDING MATERIAL IS 3/8" PLYWOOD
UNLESS OTHERWISE SPECIFIED.

(4) Cut suitable lengths of car window washer hosing, split the tubing end-to-end and apply to the upper and lower edges of the strapping. Use nylon thread or string to lace the tubing to the strapping.

(5) Drill holes on the resistor mounting plate and mount the resistors with the hardware provided with the resistors. Cut a fiberglass, bakelite, or plexiglass control panel 4¾″ × 2″ (do not use metal as it may be a shock hazard). Drill holes into the control panel to accommodate the jacks, switches, and fuse. Use Letraset to identify the control panel functions and then apply a coat of polyurethane varnish over the entire panel. Let dry. Apply red MonoKote to the control panel positive starter output and black MonoKote to the negative starter output.

(6) Install the control panel hardware. Use 18-gauge or heavier wire to connect the resistors, switches, jacks, and fuse as per the diagram. Cut two 1-foot lengths of battery lead-in wire and label

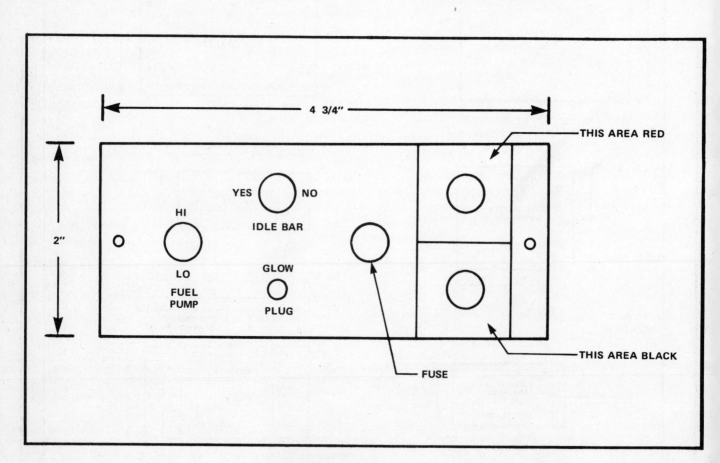

CONTROL PANEL
(ACTUAL SIZE)

the leads positive (+) and negative (−). Solder the battery lugs to the battery leads and connect as per diagram. Bolt the resistor mounting plate to the battery tray.

(7) Identify the fuel pump wires, red (+), black (−), and cut off the alligator clips. Fit the fuel pump to the box (see manufacturer's instructions) and pass the pump wires into the box through a hole drilled under the pump. Tie a knot in the fuel pump wires just where the wires enter the box and solder the wires to appropriate resistors.

(8) Slide resistor mounting plate and battery tray assembly into the battery compartment. Use screws to fasten the control panel to the box. Place the battery into the battery tray. Note: The battery has an overflow vent line. Cut a short length of Gold-N-Rod *outer* tubing, drill a hole through the battery tray and box, fit the tube to the vent line and pass the tube through the hole in the box. Connect the battery lead-in wires to the battery. Fit the carry-

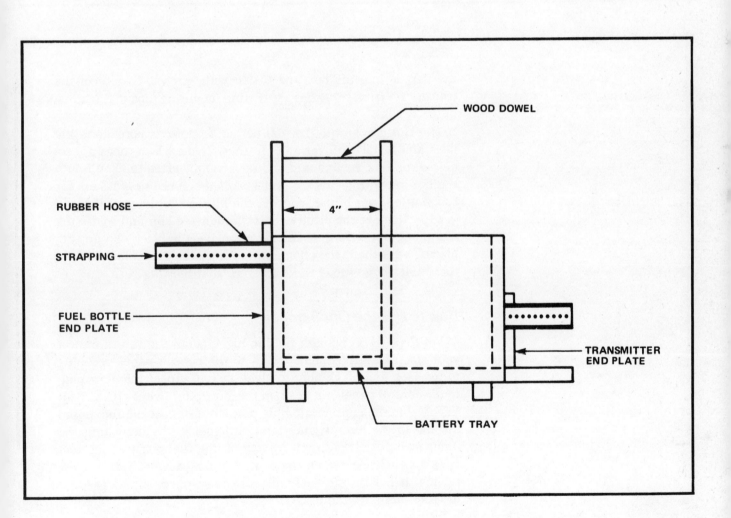

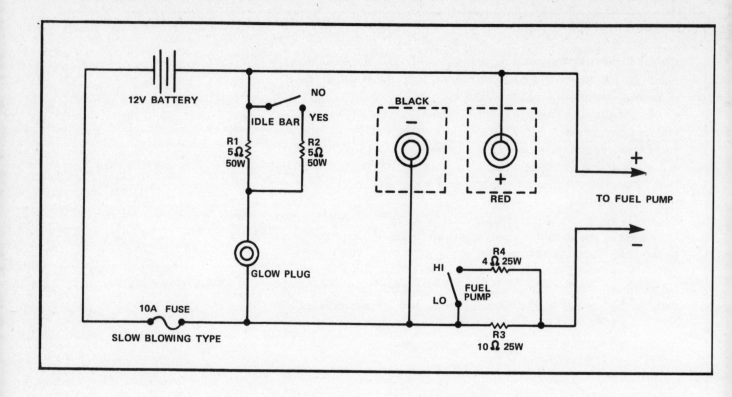

ing handle into the box and fasten with screws. To protect the transmitter from scratches apply wing mounting tape to the transmitter bracket.

(9) Cut a hole into the fuel bottle, as close as possible to the neck and install Sullivan tank fittings. (Note: Two tubes are required; one for fueling and one for a vent). Place the bottle into the box mounting bracket and install the fuel lines. When the fuel bottle is not in use, connect the fill tube to the vent line.

(10) Remove the electric starter motor red clip and solder the red phono plug. Do the same by removing the black clip and replacing with the black phono plug. Solder the glow plug cable to the small phono lug. Install 10 amp. slow-blowing fuse.

How to Use the One Tripper

Fill the fuel bottle with fuel no higher than the vent. Connect your electric starter motor cables to the control panel, red plug to red jack and black plug to black jack. Connect the glow plug to the control panel and position the glow plug switch, IDLE BAR YES/NO to the appropriate plug position. Connect the fuel pump fill line to the aircraft fuel tank and fuel up by activating the pump switch to IN (switch located on the fuel pump). The fuel HI/LO switch located on the control panel provides fast or slow fueling. If the aircraft fuel tank is to be emptied, simply position the fuel pump switch to OUT.

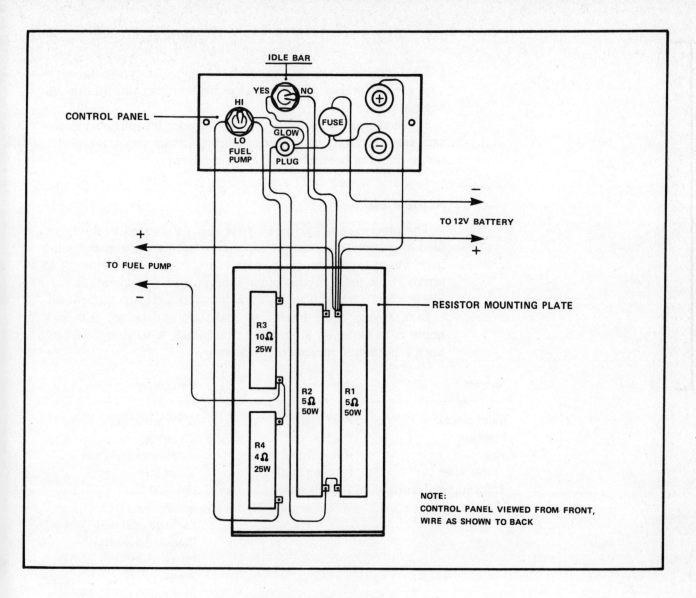

NOTE:
CONTROL PANEL VIEWED FROM FRONT,
WIRE AS SHOWN TO BACK

LIST OF PARTS

RESISTORS (Wire-Wound Fixed)

Quantity	Value	Watts	Part Number
1	5 ohms	50	R1
1	5 ohms	50	R2
1	10 ohms	25	R3
1	4 ohms	25	R4

HARDWARE

Quantity	Nomenclature
1	Fuse holder panel mounted (for ¼" x 1" fuse)
2	Switch SPST (15 amps., 125V)
1	Fuse 10 amp. (dual-element slow-blowing type)
2	Standard ¼" phone jacks (2 conductor type)
2	Standard ¼" phone plugs, black/red (2 conductor type)
1	Miniature jack (2 conductor type)
1	Miniature plug (2 conductor type)
1	12 volt motorcycle battery (5½" high by 5½" long by 3½" deep, typical)
1	Fuel pump (Sonic-Tronics "Nifty")
5 ft.	18 gauge wire (or heavier), covered, stranded
1	Fuel bottle adapter (Sullivan, Kavan)
1	80 oz. plastic bottle (Heinz vinegar bottle)
	⅜" Plywood (see detailed diagram)
	Fiberglass or plexiglass or bakelite for Control Panel (see detailed diagram)
	6" x 3¼" Aluminum for resistor mounting plate (see detail diagram)

MISCELLANEOUS

Screws—wood, flathead ¾" x 4"—Box Construction
Screws—wood, roundhead 1" x 6"—Handle and Control Panel
Strapping—(type used to support plumbing pipes)
Nuts, bolts and washers
Window washer hosing—6 feet
Wing mounting tape
Nylon thread
Battery lugs (2 required)
Wooden dowel (broom handle)
Letraset

Next, connect your glow plug connector to the glow plug, apply your electric starter motor to the propeller, start up, throttle the engine, and be ready to fly.

There is enough room in the One Tripper for all items necessary for a day's flying—electric starter motor, props, tools, etc., not to mention beer, blondes, and screwdrivers.

At the Field:

The procedure of taking all your new goodies off to the flying field may seem like a simple experience hardly worth mentioning here, but many flyers, after years of experience, still manage to arrive at the field missing some vital part of the operation . . . like a wing, a transmitter antenna, or even the transmitter itself.

Best way to avoid having to make an unexpected trip back home is to make up a checklist and attach it to your field box. Such a list would include the following:

Aircraft	Power	Maintenance
Balsa shims*	Fuel	Allen wrenches
Fuselage	Fuel pump	Cleaning fluid
Tail	Hot and cool plugs	Extra nuts and bolts
Transmitter	Priming bottle	Extra screws
Transmitter antenna	1½-volt starting battery	First aid kit
Wing	Wire and glow-clip	5-minute epoxy
		Package of Handi-Wipes
		Patching material
		Pliers
		Props
		Extra prop nut and washer
		Rags
		Razor knife
		Rubber bands
		Screwdriver
		Plug wrench
		Tape
		Wrench

* Used to make incidence changes if required.

16
Going Flying

Putting the field box on a table near the door, just read off the items on the checklist as you load the car and you'll arrive well equipped to begin the business of having fun in the air.

When loading the car, place heavy items, such as the field box, forward of where you intend to position the plane. Old blankets or towels make excellent protective packing and save a lot of dents and dinges from occurring when you might have to slam on the brakes.

When arriving at the field, don't leave everything locked in the trunk or the back of a station wagon if it's a hot day. Temperatures in such sealed areas on a normally hot summer's day can get to 140 degrees and over—all very damaging to radio, fuel, rubber, and other components. If the field is a dirty one, leave the gear in the rear, but open the trunk or windows to allow air circulation.

If you haven't as yet made contact with a club and gotten to know some of its members, and you are about to make your first visit to a club's field, there are certain laws of survival that the novice must press into practice at this juncture—one is that he must proceed *cautiously*. Don't pipe up with, "Anyone here who can help me learn to fly?" This can bring forth the club leech who never builds anything, but learns to fly with planes built by those who don't know him. Instead, practice discretion. Ask around among the assemblage as to which fellow is the best flyer on the field, and after hearing the same name three of four times, approach this hero and ask him if he would help you learn to fly when he has time. (A few words here to the effect that you have heard of his aerial prowess, and so forth, will go far in getting him to give you his undivided attention until the day *you* become the club ace. . . .)

Once you make contact with a good flyer willing to help you (most are), he will no doubht check your plane to see if all is in proper order. If he asks that something be corrected, don't stalk off to find another flyer; make the correction; it's for your own good.

You must remember not to turn on your transmitter at *any* time while at the field, unless your new mentor gives his OK— to do so will probably knock some other flyer out of the air, a messy way to get started with a new group of people in a club. Most clubs have methods of frequency control, and you should make it a point to learn the local method and strictly observe it at all times. The majority of clubs use color-coded clothespins, but since the practice varies across the country, I leave it to you to get this procedure directly from the fellows you will fly with, just as I hesitate to enter into the procedure of actual flying methods since your flying instructor will have his own methods to guide you and these will be far more valuable than words in a book.

Hopefully you will be in a position to follow through on a club contact to arrange your flying lessons and further field check-out procedures. If not, we will assume that you are in the midst of nowhere and need the written word as guidance and proceed from there.

On the above assumption, you arrive at a lonely flying site that you have chosen in order to teach yourself to fly. You have a smooth, flat surface of cement, asphalt, clay, or closely mowed grass that is approximately 200 feet in diameter or larger, and there are no trees or other obstructions close to this selected take-off/landing area. Your time of arrival should coincide with the local weather conditions, i.e., little, if any wind (normally early morning and late evening), and, if you are *absolutely* certain that no one is flying within 5 miles of your chosen site, you are ready to begin. However, take time to practice caution in face of the fact that someone else may have the same idea as you and also be out at the same time on what he too believes to be a lonely location. To test your "aloneness" turn on your plane's receiver, NOT the *transmitter,* and see if you receive any signals to any surfaces. Try this for 1 to 2 minutes at a time over a 15- to 20-minute period, leaving the set off for around 3 to 5 minutes at a time. This test should be run with the plane held high overhead so that the receiver may adequately pick up any transmitted signals for you to see. If none are seen you are ready to try your first test hop— *after* you repeat the at-home test procedure to see that all surfaces

are properly aligned, all surfaces answer to proper commands (double-checking to see that right is right, left is left, and so on), and the engine runs up and responds to throttle controls from transmitter. Check to be sure that all surfaces are at neutral with no control from the transmitter, and not slightly UP/DOWN— RIGHT/LEFT, and so forth. This is VITAL! Correct discrepancies with the clevis pins, and *not* by use of the transmitter trim controls.

Your engine should be carrying a low-pitch prop in the 3- to 4-inch range so that you do not have to fight a torque situation. Again, this means if your engine calls for a 10-inch prop, it should be one designated as 10×3 inches, or 10×4 inches. (Or your engine may call for an 11- or 12-inch prop: 11×3, 11×4; 12×3, 12×4; and so on.)

Your engine should not be tuned to a screaming crescendo for your first flights. Tune it to scream, then back off on the needle valve to a slightly rich setting and tilt the nose of the plane straight up. If you have the setting right, the engine will continue to run. If too lean, or too rich, the engine will stop, start over, and readjust.

Set the engine to low throttle and back away from the plane, being sure the nose is pointed directly into the wind. Give a control command to each surface to be sure all of them function, and if all checks out, you are ready to fly, or become of a member of the CAF (Chicken Air Force—its members *never* fly).

Ease the throttle control full forward and give the rudder a slight bit of right to offset the thrust surge. If your plane is properly aligned and balanced, it will take off with no help from you, and in fact should have no help from you if you can resist the urge to wiggle sticks. A little control usually goes a long way, so be *gentle* in your stick handling. Also, never point the transmitter antenna directly at your plane. This results in possible loss of signal. Keep the antenna parallel to the flight path or aimed away from the plane.

Once the plane breaks from the ground and has traveled about 25 to 50 feet, a slight bit of elevator-*up* control can be given. You will no doubt expect instant results, and, seeing none apparent, will wish to feed in more up control. *Don't!* The beginner expects instant action and therefore tends to overcontrol, then quickly finds himself in desperate trouble. Go slowly and gently and give your plane time to respond. It really responds much quicker than the novice thinks.

After attaining a good amount of altitude (100 to 200 feet), you are ready to try your first turn. Since an airplane loses altitude in a turn and therefore picks up speed, the situation presented to the beginner can be hair-raising as he tries to figure out what to do with his berserk charge. Therefore, throttle back to half throttle *before* applying rudder. This will keep your speed down, which in turn allows more time to think. As you apply rudder, a slight bit of up elevator is also applied to keep the nose up, again using both controls by small degrees. Because the engine is throttled back, control response will be slow, so don't force more control if you don't see instant action.

Once your first turn is completed leave the engine in low throttle and fly a series of "Indianapolis turns"—large open turns to gain further experience with the controls. While doing these turns, keep the main flight path of the plane on a course at right angles to the wind and upwind of your position.

As the plane comes toward you, the rudder control will be reversed. Most beginners turn around to face in the direction of the plane's flight in order to avoid confusion. Instead of doing this, remember that when the plane comes toward you, you will push the stick in the same direction as the plane is turning in order to correct the turn and get the plane back to straight flight.

Your next maneuver, like it or not, is the landing, and it is performed much like the Indianapolis turns, only the throttle control is pulled all the way back so the engine is running at its lowest rpm level. Make a run downwind, a turn to go cross-wind, and a final turn into the wind about 200 to 300 feet away from your intended landing place. On each turn, do not feed in any up-elevator—you *want* to lose altitude on each turn so that on the final approach you will be dropping at a normal sink speed to your landing. Once the plane is near the landing spot, gently pull the stick back for up-elevator. This is to get the nose up for a final near-stall as the plane is ready to touch down. Just at touchdown, pull the stick all the way back and keep it there to keep the tail down. Don't expect perfection here—it takes some time to learn the "feeling" of when to make a turn and how far you can stretch the glide back to earth. There too, each plane is different and has its own sink speed. For this reason, you will want to begin a pattern of practice that includes a great number of "touch-and-goes"—landings with no stop that go into an immediate takeoff, flight around the field and in for another touch-and-go.

This repetitive practice, although you may think it dull, sharpens your senses, perfects your flying, and will allow you to become so adept that you may go on to become world champion. Even if the big hardware doesn't interest you, repetitive practice will soon have you in the position where you can handle any panic situation automatically.

I've purposely made no mention of any aerobatics. This is not an attempt to shortchange you. Too many beginners hear how a roll, Immelman, and the like are done and lunge right into trying their hand at it before they know the basics of flight and how to get their planes back on course without panic. The result, nine times out of 10, is demolished airplane and equipment. As in full-size flying, learn the basics well, then take your aerobatic course from someone who can stand beside you and correct mistakes as they happen, so mistakes do not become habits.

In your beginning days you will probably have innumerable hard landings. After each, be sure to run through an extremely thorough plane and equipment check-out, with and without the engine running. Check alignments, surface settings, engine and fuel system—the works, just as though you were checking out a whole new airplane. This is called longevity insurance—ignore it and you'll go from one stunning smashup to the next on a highly regular basis. Not only stupid, but highly costly. So use your head and be thorough in your approach to R/C and you'll enjoy it immensely.

17
Radio Care

Since radio equipment is your one single most expensive investment, you of course want to treat it with respect. However, the radio is also responsible for the safety and care of the planes you build—another reason to treat the entire unit with even more love and attention.

When you receive your new radio, don't leave it lying around on your workbench while you build the plane it will be used with. Servos in particular are highly susceptible to dirt, and the balsa dust alone in any modeler's shop is enough to do serious damage to these units. Keep the radio gear in a closed box until you're ready to make equipment installations, and even after these installations are made, keep the receiver and servos protected by some sort of covering that will keep dust out. The same applies to the transmitter. Keep it covered and clean at all times.

Once the plane is completed, take the same cleanliness precautions. Don't store your model where dust can collect in and on servos or receiver, and don't let it sit at the flying site where all sorts of dirt can make its way inside the fuselage to infest these same vital parts! Your transmitter should also be well protected before, during, and after use. After a trip to the field, the transmitter, in particular, should be well cleaned on the exterior with alcohol to remove fuel residue from handling. While at the field, try to avoid leaving the transmitter where dirt can get into it, and by all means keep it out of the prop blast of all engines to avoid fuel getting inside.

If you fly weekly, once a month carefully examine all wiring for chafing signs, cracks, fraying, or similar signs of wear. Check servo wheels to see that screws are still snug and do the same with servo mounts. Check push rod connections to be sure that they are still firmly mounted.

Before each flight, the antenna on the *transmitter* should be checked for snugness of fit. A number of flyers have ignored this one—to have their antenna fall off while the plane is in flight. The *aircraft* antenna should also be checked before each flight to be sure it isn't coiled inside the plane, and on the monthly inspection it should be checked for breaks or signs of wear, especially at the point it exits from the fuselage.

A most important part of radio care is proper maintenance of transmitter and airborne batteries. There are innumerable theories as to the care and feeding of the nickel cadmium battery but the following, excerpted from the book *R/C Modeler's Flight Training Course,* would seem to express the majority opinion in the United States:

A nickel cadmium battery is certainly the cause of a great percentage of "problems" in radios sent back to the manufacturer for repair. A good number of the problems with nickel cadmium batteries could be eliminated by following a few simple procedures.

First of all, charge the radio for 24 hours, per the manufacturer's instructions, before operating your new radio for the first time. Second, after your normal day's flying, regardless of the number of flights you have made, charge your radio overnight with the manufacturer's charger, and then store your aircraft with the fully charged batteries ready for the next flying session. Third, if you don't fly your model during the next week, charge the batteries for at least 8 hours before going to fly. If your equipment has not been used for 4 to 6 weeks, a full overnight charge should be given.

Since most flyers do not completely discharge their batteries during a normal flying session, a normal charge time of 8 to 12 hours is more than adequate. If, however, you are one of those air hogs who has flown for the maximum time allotted for your nickel cadmium batteries [1½ to 2 hours], we recommend the full overnight charge of 16 to 20 hours.

A good point to note when charging your batteries is that the charging indicator lights located on your charger (if the charger is separate from the transmitter) or on the transmitter case itself (if the charger is located inside the transmitter) is lit when the system is plugged in. Nothing is more frustrating than to assume that you have put your batteries on charge all night, only to find the next day that the charger, in fact, was not charging at all simply because you had improperly plugged in the charging receptacles.

There have been all types of technical articles published in *R/CM*, as well as the other model publications, on "cycling" your nickel cadmium batteries, and specialized chargers and dischargers designed for their use. While these articles are primarily of interest for the technically orientated, we have never used one of these devices ourselves, and have simply followed the manufacturer's instructions for the care and charging of the nickel cadmium batteries suppied with each proportional system. Over the last 9 years of editing *R/C Modeler Magazine*, we have flown and tested virtually every known type of proportional system, and during that time have had only one battery failure due to a defective nickel cadmium cell. By following the manufacturer's instructions for charging nickel cadmium batteries accompanying his proportional system, you'll not encounter any difficulties with your nickel cadmium packs unless a cell is defective.

18
Some Common Sense

Too many people who enter the fascinating hobby of R/C regard the planes they fly as "toys," or they equate these sophisticated flying drones with "model airplanes." A radio-controlled plane is neither toy nor model—it is a full-fledged flying machine, traveling at speeds up to 160 mph, with weights in excess of 4 pounds, and hence a potential killer in the hands of an idiot.

A beginner, flying in crowded areas without proper guidance, or trying to impress people by flying low over their heads, is a manifold idiot; and the one who tries his luck at coming close to a full-size plane in flight is one to be committed to an institution for the criminally insane.

In short, R/C is a great deal of fun if you go into it sensibly. Through a tremendous amount of effort by the Academy of Model Aeronautics, R/C flyers enjoy a great deal of freedom that might not otherwise exist. The FAA (Federal Aviation Authority) is keeping a close eye on R/C flyers as a potential hazard to commercial aviation and, although no stringent laws have been passed to govern R/C flying, the Academy has garnered a gentlemen's agreement with FAA that no R/C plane should be flown over 400 feet within 3 miles of an airport. If a contest is to be held within this 3-mile range, the hosting club calls the control tower operator and informs him of the club's intentions. For an individual to violate this pleasant and workable agreement through his own selfishness will have the local club out looking for him—and their normal treatment of such an individual makes the Mafia look like good guys!

The AMA Safety Code is one every flyer should observe, and it goes like this:

OFFICIAL AMA SAFETY CODE

GENERAL

1. I will not fly my model aircraft in competition or in the presence of spectators until it has been proven to be airworthy by having been previously successfully flight tested.

2. I will not fly my model higher than approximately 400 feet within 3 miles of an airport, without notifying the airport operator. I will give right of way to, and avoid flying in the proximity of, full scale aircraft. Where necessary, an observer shall be utilized to supervise flying to avoid having models fly in the proximity of full scale aircraft.

3. Where established, I will abide by the safety rules for the flying site I use, and I will not willfully and deliberately fly my models in a careless, reckless, and/or dangerous manner.

RADIO CONTROL

1. I will have completed a successful radio equipment ground range check before the first flight of a new or repaired model.

2. I will not fly my model aircraft in the presence of spectators until I become a qualified flyer, unless assisted by an experienced helper.

3. I will perform my initial turn after takeoff away from the pit, spectator, and parking areas, and I will not thereafter perform maneuvers, flights of any sort, or landing approaches over a pit, spectator, or parking area.

Other than using common sense when flying near an airport or people, the R/C flyer needs to observe some other basics that will insure his not hitting someone or something—or wiping out his own equipment—should he be selfish enough to think only of himself. An excerpt from *R/C Modeler*, as written by Don Dewey, the editor, sums this up quite well:

When you are airborne at the local flying field and you get a 'glitch' . . . that is, a sudden reaction of the aircraft which was not caused by the loose nut on the transmitter, it could be a sudden gust of wind . . . or it could be radio interference or a sudden malfunction of your radio equipment. Don't try to "second guess" the nature of the problem! Instantly, set up for your landing approach, throttle back and land the aircraft! Do not attempt to 'fly through' the interference, or simply hope that the unexplained glitch will go away. A failure to heed this warning sign is very much similar to a person who develops a toothache and refuses to go to the dentist, rationalizing that, when he wakes up in the morning, the toothache will be gone!

Certainly, we go to the field to fly. And the thought of having to land your aircraft and wait an indeterminate period of time in order to fly again, or possibly not at all, is not to your liking. But it would be far less to your liking to have the intermittent glitch turn into a sudden massive failure of the radio system causing the loss of your aircraft and radio and possibly damage to someone else's equipment or person. Thus, we repeat: If you experience an unexpected interruption of your flight from an unknown source, land the aircraft at once.

Once on the ground, check your battery voltage if you have a volt meter in your field box. Check to make sure that you don't have loose connections between your servos and receiver, or between your control surfaces and the push rods. Check to make sure that none of your equipment has shifted position or come loose from its foam rubber packing. Check the servos to make sure that you have not compressed the servo grommets too tightly against the servo tray. Make certain that you do not have any metal-to-metal joints that could be causing electrical noise to interfere with the receiver.

If you encounter any one of these problems, the remedy is quite simple—correct it and then check your aircraft out completely with a pre-flight check-out as previously illustrated.

Since the average modeler does not carry a volt meter with him, checking the condition of the nickel cadmium batteries can be something of a problem. One simple check is to operate the controls and make sure that they do not move more slowly in one direction than in another. If they do, and your surfaces are not binding, it is a good indication of weak cells in your nickel cadmium pack. Check your transmitter, too, to make sure that the RF indicator on the transmitter meter is in whatever position it normally is for flying. In some transmitters, this may be on the full right hand side of the meter, or someplace in between. If there is a substantial difference between the position of the needle on your meter [and] where it is when you normally fly, it is a good indication that there is something wrong with the nickel cadmium batteries in the transmitter. Another good idea would be to collapse the antenna and carry out a range check on the ground to make sure that you have adequate range. If you do not, this is another possible indication that you may have trouble with your battery pack.

Check your receiver antenna where it exits the receiver and where it exits the fuselage. Make sure that you have not torn the insulation on the receiver antenna where it exits the side of the fuselage, and that you have not exerted so much strain on the antenna that you have pulled it loose from the receiver. Follow this up by checking each servo and making sure that they are neither too tight nor too loose on their mounts. The servo grommets should not be compressed and the servos should be allowed to just move slightly when moved with a finger. If they are too tight, or conversely, too loose, the problem could be one of vibration being transmitted to the servo due to improper mounting. Check to make sure that the servo cables or receiver wire have not become entangled with the servos themselves, or even worse, with the push rod wires.

If you have located the problem by this check-out process, and you can successfully rectify it at the field, check the plane out thoroughly for proper control surface movement both with the engine running and not running. Make sure that everything is operating properly before you fuel up, fire up the engine, and rush out for another flight. Do not assume that you have found the complete problem—make sure that no further problem exists before taking off and commencing another flight.

If you did not locate the problem, and the problem does not reappear with the plane on the ground, either with or without the engine running, the problem may have been one of radio interference. Check with other flyers at the field (if there are any) and see if they have been experiencing any interference on their frequencies. If you are fortunate enough to have another flyer in the area on your same frequency, ask him if he has had any difficulties, or if he has not yet flown, warn him of the problems you had, mentioning that it could possibly be radio interference, and wait a period of time before either of you attempt to fly again. If he does decide to fly, watch his flight carefully and see if he experiences any difficulties similar to your own. Obviously, the use of a field monitor would be ideal since it could monitor all of the frequencies. Plans for such monitors have been presented in *R/C Modeler Magazine* as well as other publications. Oftentimes the local flying club will have a monitor at the field in order to check the frequencies for any possible interference or to monitor a given frequency when interference is suspected. If you have a duel frequency system (usually the frequencies are widely separated), and if interference is experienced on one frequency, it is only necessary to switch the transmitter and receiver switches to the opposing frequency. Usually no further problems will result. In some cases, one particular frequency may be the source of continuous interference from some industrial transmission in a given area. For example, 27.045 mHz may be a "bad" frequency in one given area while it is perfectly suitable in another. Check with your local flying club and find out if they have a frequency problem on one or more frequencies.

Quite often, industrial transmissions from a nearby source are quite powerful and may swamp the entire model band. This is usually not the case with a local flying field since this aspect of operation has usually been thoroughly checked out before the flying field was established. However, if you are flying by yourself, you may be adjacent to an industrial transmission source of which you were unaware. If you are close enough, all the model frequencies may be swamped-out completely by this transmission. So, all that remains for you to do is to find another flying site.

Another problem is the widespread and continuing illegal use of the Class D Citizens' Band radios by Citizens' Band operators. It is rather frightening to turn on a CB radio and listen to individuals calling each other without the use of assigned call letters, using bootleg names, and boasting of the fact that they are using 500 watt linear amplifiers on a Class D radio station that is authorized for a maximum output of 5 watts only. Unfortunately, there is very little that we can do about this situation except to inform the Federal Communications [Commission] field office nearest you, when a violator has been heard. Unfortunately, it is extremely difficult to track down these violators, since location is almost impossible to determine due to their deliberate lack of use of call letters. In many cases, these are mobile operators moving from place to place and using Class D Citizens' Radio Service as a playground for their own illegal activities simply to avoid having to take a code and theory test in order to obtain an Amateur Radio Operator's License where they could talk to their heart's content within the limits prescribed for the amateur radio service. If you discover a Citizens' Band operator who is deliberately attempting to "shoot your aircraft down" do not take matters into your own hands! There is a serious penalty, and possible imprisonment, for damaging the equipment or impairing the transmission of a Citizens' Band or Amateur Radio system. Let the Federal Communications Commission handle your complaint, but if you are complaining, make sure that you have enough facts to back up that complaint. The FCC, like all federal agencies, is quite busy and has its hands full with more important problems. They will be more than happy to assist you if they can, but need all the facts and data that you can possibly provide them as to the source of illegal interference.

Remember, we are sharing the radio waves with legal Citizens' Band operators, medical services, and industrial transmission. We have a right to the frequencies assigned to us within the limits prescribed by the Federal Communications Commission. So do these other users have a legal right to the air waves within the parameters prescribed for them by the FCC. It is only the illegal operators, whether they be Class D Citizens' Band operators or radio control enthusiasts operating on an illegal frequency or outside the limits prescribed for the operation of their equipment, that cause us all difficulties.

GLOSSARY

In the present state of the art, it is not necessary to know any of the "inside" language of radio in order to enjoy R/C to the fullest extent. However, the curious will want an inkling of what the jargon at the flying field is all about, so I list the following most often used terms. (A good number of these terms have been excerpted from *R/C Modeler Flight Training Course.*)

AILERON: The movable portion of the wing of the aircraft which causes a change in the roll mode of the aircraft.

AIR BLEED: An adjustment screw on the carburetor of a model engine allowing a micrometer-like adjustment of air into the venturi.

AIRBORNE BATTERY PACK: The batteries used to power the receiver-decoder and servos in the aircraft.

AIRFOIL: The cross-section of a wing if cut chord-wise through the wing.

AIR LOADS: Referring to the load imposed upon an aircraft while moving through the air or prescribing maneuvers during flight.

AIR SCOOP: An opening in an aircraft designed to direct air to the interior of the aircraft.

ALKALINE ENERGIZER: A particular type of dry battery in various sizes which is not normally rechargeable.

ALUMINUM OXIDE PAPER: A type of sandpaper which allows very little residue build-up.

AMA: Academy of Model Aeronautics. The governing body of Model aviation in America, and the world's largest sport aviation organization. Over two-thirds of AMA membership are adults.

ANTENNA: The vertical antenna is located on top of the transmitter and must be extended for flying. The receiving antenna exits the fuselage and is usually attached to the top of the vertical fin on the aircraft.

ARF: An abbreviation used to indicate an "almost-ready-to-fly" aircraft kit.

AUTOGYRO: A type of aircraft which uses a conventional engine for forward speed and a nonpowered rotating set of blades above the aircraft which create lift and enable the autogyro to ascend and descend in a confined area.

AXIS: A center point about which an aircraft moves, such as yaw, roll, or pitch axis.

BALLAST: Weight used in a model aircraft to adjust the aircraft to the proper center of gravity [or, CG].

BAND: Referring to a frequency band such as 27 mHz or 72 mHz.

BATS: Batteries.

BAYS: Normally used as in "wing bays," the area between ribs on an aircraft wing.

BEAM MOUNTS: Horizontal members in the nose of an aircraft made of hardwood or metal on which the engine is mounted.

BELLCRANK: A nylon lever used between the servo and a control surface to convert the movement of the servo at right angles to the servo output. Bellcranks are usually available in 60- and 120-degree modes.

BENT: Same as "dingled."

BLOCK-UP: To raise a structure above a flat surface.

BLUSH: A condition where freshly painted dope loses its shine and takes on a "milky" color due to being applied in cold and/or wet weather.

BUDDY BOX: A method used to train new flyers wherein a slave transmitter is plugged into the instructor's master transmitter allowing the instructor to override the student's control actions.

BUILDING DIRT: Any loose material left within an airplane prior to covering. This material will set up strange noises, or "hums," when a plane is in flight.

BULKHEAD: Structural members of the fuselage normally made of plywood or balsa.

BUTT-JOINT: A joint wherein the ends of two lengths of balsa or hardwood are joined together.

BUTYRATE: A type of aircraft dope that is impervious to most fuels used in model aircraft engines.

CABANE STRUTS: Normally used to refer to the upper wing supports for a biplane, but also the wing supports projecting from the fuselage and attached to the underside of high-winged aircraft.

CABIN: That portion of the aircraft simulating a cockpit and passenger area of a full-size high-winged aircraft. This area is normally used on an R/C model for housing the radio equipment.

CAF: "Chicken Air Force"—comprised of those too terrified to fly their creations. (Its one time, and present, members are legion!)

CAM-LOK: Full-size aircraft fastener used by some modelers to attach wings to fuselage.

CANOPY: Normally, a tear-drop-shaped plastic cockpit enclosure.

CAPSTRIPS: Thin strips of balsa glued to the top and/or bottom of wing ribs to provide additional strength to the wing as well as to provide a larger surface to which the wing covering may adhere.

CENTERLINE: A line drawn down the center, e.g., such as a line drawn down the dead center of a fuselage or down the center of a bulkhead.

CHICKEN STICK: A term used to indicate a short length of material used for flipping a propeller when starting in order to protect the fingers from harm.

CHOKING: Placing a finger over the venturi of an engine while starting in order to increase the initial fuel flow to the engine.

CHOPPER: Slang terminology for a helicopter.

CHORD: The measurement from the leading edge to the trailing edge of the wing.

CG: Center of gravity.

CLEVIS: A device on the end of a push rod to attach the push rod to a control horn at the control surface.

CLUNK TANK: A model aircraft fuel tank, so-called because of the flexible fuel line with a weighted pick-up tube which enables the fuel line to fall, or "clunk," to any part of the tank, thus picking up fuel despite the attitude of the aircraft. (Also "klunk.")

COLD JOINT: A solder connection made with insufficient heat and therefore highly subject to quick vibration fatigue and failure.

COMPOUND CURVE: A surface which curves in more than one direction.

COMPRESSION SCREW: The adjustment on the head of a diesel engine for varying the compression of the engine. (Diesel engines are not normally used in R/C.)

CONTROL HORN: A small nylon fitting mounted on the control surface to which the push rod clevis is attached providing a mechanical connection between the push rod and the control surface in order to move that surface.

CONTROL SURFACE: A movable portion of the aircraft which, when deflected, alters the flight attitude of the aircraft.

CONVENTIONAL GEAR: Used to indicate an aircraft with main gear and either steerable or fixed tail wheel.

COWL: The forward-most part of the aircraft's fuselage normally enclosing the engine.

CRAB: A plane flying at an angle to its path over the ground due to high-wind conditions.

CRANK: A bellcrank used to change the direction of a servo's thrust.

CREAMED: Worse than bent or dingled.

CROSS-WIND: A wind that blows at right or oblique angles to the direction of flight.

DEAD STICK: For example, landing dead stick, the engine having quit during the flight, requiring the aircraft to be landed without benefit of throttle.

DECALAGE: Referring to the angular settings of the wing stabilizer in reference to a common datum line.

DECIBEL RATING: A method of rating the noise level of a model aircraft engine using a meter at a prescribed distance from that engine.

DIAGONALS: Referring to secondary bracing used in a model aircraft such as the diagonal bracing between two longerons and a fuselage side.

DIE-CUT: Referring to method of machine cutting of kit parts wherein the parts are cut all the way through a sheet of balsa or plywood but more often remain in that sheet to be removed by the builder.

DIESEL ENGINE: A model aircraft engine with variable compression which burns ether-based fuel and fires on compression alone without glow plug or starting battery.

DIGITAL: Referring to a digital proportional radio control system.

DIHEDRAL: The upward rake of each wing panel to provide "built-in" stability.

DIHEDRAL BRACE: A plywood or balsa brace used at the dihedral joint to support that section from stress and breakage.

DINGLED: Cracked-up, but repairable.

DIRIGIBLE: A lighter-than-air craft.

DISPLACEMENT: The volume swept by the piston in a model engine; the bore multiplied by the stroke and used as an index of comparative engine size.

DOPE: The fast-drying paint used on aircraft.

DORSAL: The small portion of the vertical fin which fairs into the top of the fuselage.

DOUBLE GLUING: A method of cementing balsa wood joints for extra strength wherein the glue is applied to each surface and allowed to dry before the parts are glued in place using a second application of glue or cement.

DOWEL: A length of hardwood formed in a round shape available in various diameters from ⅛ inch to 1 inch or more; ³⁄₁₆- and ¼-inch-diameter dowels are often used with shaped wire ends as push rods.

DOWN-ELEVATOR: The deflection of the elevator in the down position, causing the aircraft to change its pitch mode.

DOWN-WIND: Flying in a direction opposite to that from which the wind is coming.

DRAG: A force exerted against the direction of flight by the resistance of the air.

DURAL: Referring to dural aluminum used normally for landing gear on a shoulder or high-wing model.

ELEVATOR: The movable portion of the aircraft attached to the horizontal stabilizer which, when moved, creates a change in pitch of the aircraft.

ELEVEN METER: Referring to a frequency band used by amateur radio operators on which are several spot frequencies that can be used by RC'ers holding a Technician's Class License.

ENGINE BEARERS: Lengths of hardwood on which the engine is mounted in the engine compartment.

EXHAUST BUTTERFLY: A flat metal plate which is coupled to the throttle arm on the carburetor and closes over the exhaust port as the engine is idled down, thus causing back pressure inside the engine, thereby aiding the engine to idle properly.

FAI: Fédération Aeronatique Internationale, the governing body for all forms of sport aviation throughout the world, including modeling.

FAIL-SAFE: An electronic device in some radio systems which automatically returns a servo, or servos, to neutral in case of radio malfunction or interference.

FAIRING: A smooth and streamline transition from one external surface to another.

FCC: Federal Communications Commission, the federal agency assigned to the control and regulation of all radio transmissions.

FEEDBACK: Not in common use today but still around. Refers to receiver being too close to transmitter and sending signals back to jam transmission. A microphone too close to an amplifier will also give feedback in the form of a howl.

FIELDBOX: The box of equipment needed at the flying field.

FIGURE 9, FIGURE 7: Aerobatics contain the maneuver, "figure 8," two concentric circles flown horizontally or vertically. Picture the figure 7 or 9 flown with the maneuver ending at the tail of the maneuver—in the ground. (A once-in-an-airplane maneuver; try to avoid either.)

FILAMENT: For example, monofilament tape, a high-strength, adhesive-backed tape composed of single strands of fiberglass or other material rendering the tape almost impervious to cross tearing.

FILLET: A rounded joint between two right-angle surfaces.

FIN: Referring to the vertical stabilizer.

FIREWALL: A plywood bulkhead located directly behind the engine.

FIXED LANDING GEAR: Landing gear which is nonretractable.

FLAPERON: A term used to describe a combination control wherein both aileron and flap action are obtained from a single control surface.

FLAPS: Panels hinged to the lower surface of the wing which, when lowered, can increase lift and reduce speed.

FLOATER: A plane that has an exceptionally flat glide and seemingly hates to land.

FLOATS: Landing gear used for takeoff and landing on water, e.g., pontoons.

FLUX: A material applied to the joint to be soldered in order to promote fusion.

FLYING SPEED: The velocity necessary to enable a model to lift free of earth and maintain flight.

FLYING SURFACES: The elevator, wing, rudder, and other portions of the aircraft which contribute to the support of the model in flight.

FLYING WING: A rectangular or delta-shaped model consisting primarily of a wing without the normal or conventional fuselage and tail surfaces.

FRAMEWORK: The basic structure of a model.

FREQUENCY: Each radio system operates on one of several FCC-assigned frequencies in the 27- through 72-mHz bands.

FUELPROOF: Referring to a material which is insoluble in a methyl alcohol-based fuel.

FUEL PUMP: A mechanical or electrical device used for pumping fuel from the fuel can into the fuel tank of the aircraft.

FUEL TUBING: A silicone or other type flexible tubing through which the fuel travels from the fuel tanks to the engine.

FULL-HOUSE: A slang term used to indicate an aircraft with control of all primary functions—roll, yaw, pitch, and throttle.

FUSE: Short for fuselage.

GARNET PAPER: A type of sandpaper used in model aircraft construction.

GEAR: Two meanings: 1. landing gear; 2. all the equipment one takes to the flying field.

GEAR TRAIN: A matched set of gears such as those used in a servo so mounted that each gear drives the next gear in line.

GLITCH: Means a strange twitch as the plane is flying—one not caused by the pilot, but by possible nearby radio interference. If an *honest* glitch is observed more than once in a flight, best procedure is to land at once.

GLOW PLUG: An ignition device in the cylinder head of the model engine which employs a filament which is heated for starting by means of a battery. After the engine is running, the heat of the combustion keeps the filament hot.

GOODYEAR: The trade name of a national manufacturing company which once sponsored the famous full-size Goodyear racers, small-sized racing aircraft with 65-hp engines. (In R/C, this applies to miniature copies of these famous planes. See pylon.)

GROMMET: A small rubber "donut" which is used on servos to aid in shock absorption.

GROUND LOOP: A condition wherein the aircraft, while taxiing, or landing, describes a flat circle on the ground by pivoting on one wheel.

GUSSET: A triangular-shaped piece of wood used for joint reinforcement.

HALF-A: A term that originated in early free-flight days and carried over into radio control referring to an aircraft with a .049 to .051 engine displacement.

HARDWOOD: Referring to spruce, pine, and all wood other than balsa.

HATCH: As in "balsa hatch," as used to cover an opening in a model such as for access to radio control equipment or to the fuel compartment.

HEAD-WIND: A wind blowing in the direction opposite to the flight path of the aircraft.

HIGH ASPECT RATIO: Indicating a wing that utilizes a greater than normal span with relation to the chord, or width, of the wing.

HI-START: A catapult system of launching R/C gliders. System varies, but is basically about 200 feet of high-reflex shock cord combined with about 300 feet of high-test (45- to 90-pound) nylon fishing line, with one end anchored in the ground and the other attached to the glider by means of a ring on the line over a hook on the bottom of the glider. This catapult is stretched out to its maximum, the glider attached, and then the glider is released into the wind. A high start unit will take a glider up to over 500 feet, where the hook automatically releases and the glider is on its own, under further direction from the earth-bound pilot.

HIGH-WING: Describing an aircraft with the wing mounted on top of a cabin.

HOLD-DOWN DOWELS: Short lengths of dowels passing through the fuselage near the leading and trailing edges of the wings to which hold-down rubber bands are secured to hold the wing in place during flight.

HOME BREW: A slang term referring to model glow fuel mixed by the individual modeler from his own basic ingredients.

HORN: Control horns. Term applied to the molded units attached to control surfaces to which the clevis pin or other push-rod fitting is secured.

HUNTING: Used to describe a plane's flight pattern. In contrast to smooth flight, the plane, like a dog on a trail, is searching its path. Assuming the pilot innocent, this can be due to fast-paced glitches or a badly designed or built airplane with inherent stability problems. If you have a consistent hunter, find an experienced flyer and ask his advice in solving the problem.

ID: Inside diameter, used as a reference of measurement for the inside clearance of a piece of tubing exclusive of the wall thickness of that tubing.

IF: Intermediate frequency.

IMPOUND: Place where transmitters are kept during most contests. Some large clubs also impound transmitters during normal flying sessions to avoid conflict of frequencies.

INCIDENCE: The angle formed between the chord of the wing and the datum line of the fuselage.

INHERENT STABILITY: Referring to a condition where the design of the aircraft is such that it has a tendency to right itself to a stable flight attitude when controls are neutralized.

IN-LINE FILTER: A fuel filter consisting of a small chamber and filtering screen designed to be inserted in the fuel line between the engine and fuel tank.

INVERTED ENGINE: An engine mounted with the cylinder head pointing downward instead of being mounted in the normal upright position.

JIGS: Such as a wing or fuselage jig, designed to hold a part or structure while it is being fabricated.

kHz: KiloHertz—1,000 cycles per second.

KEEPER: Any device that prevents a clevis pin or other connection from coming loose. (Commercially available.)

KNOCK-OFF: Any part of an aircraft that is designed to separate from the model in the event of a crash.

KWIK-LINK: See snap link.

LE: Leading edge, referring to the leading edge of the wing of an aircraft.

LG: Landing gear.

LIFT: The upward force exerted by the wing.

LINKAGES: Normally used to indicate a connection between a push rod and control horn or a push rod and a servo.

LONGERONS: Primary structural members of a fuselage running fore and aft in the fuselage.

LOW-ASPECT RATIO: Indicating a wing span with a lower than normal span in relationship to the chord, or width, of the wing.

MAH: Milliampere hour.

MASTER'S: "Master's Tournament," held biannually at a predetermined point in the United States, this is to choose the R/C Team to compete at the R/C Aerobatic World Championships the following year. The American team is decided from the top contest flyers in the country and is composed of the three top-score men at the Master's. Previous United States team members are automatically included in Master's competition, as are the top three Nats winners. (See "Nats.")

MHz: MegaHertz—1,000,000 cycles per second.

MOTOR RUN: The length of time an engine operates during a given flight, or on a measured tank of gas.

MPH: Miles per hour.

NATS: The Grand National Model Airplane championships, held once yearly in a predetermined section of the United States, run by AMA, and cohosted with the Navy from 1948 to 1972. Military expenditure cutbacks forced the Navy to bow out in 1972 and AMA now runs the Nats on its own. The Nats attracts over 2,000 contestants in all forms of modeling, close to one-third of whom are R/C enthusiasts.

NEEDLE VALVE: The fuel feed adjustment located on the venturi of a model engine.

NEEDLE VALVE SETTINGS: The adjustments of the glow-plug engine needle valve.

NICAD: Trade name, but all nickel cadmium batteries are referred to by it. These batteries are rechargeable and have been adopted by the R/C fraternity as the most reliable and cheapest in the long run.

NOSE BLOCK: A block, or blocks, of wood, used to form the nose area around and/or under the engine on the fuselage of a model aircraft.

NOSEGEAR: A fixed or steerable single wheel located on the front or rear of the firewall.

NOSE MOMENT: The distance from the center of gravity (CG) to the nose of the model.

NOSE WHEEL: The wheel used on the steerable, or fixed, nosegear.

OD: Outside diameter, usually used as a reference of measure for tubing.

OVER-CONTROL: The excessive amount of control by the R/C pilot resulting in an erratic movement of the aircraft.

PARASITIC DRAG: Drag caused by a built-in condition of the aircraft, such as a rough exterior surface.

PENETRATION: A plane is said to be a "good penetrator," if it flies well *into* the wind.

PIANO WIRE: Wire, available in varying diameters, used for forming push rods and landing gear.

PITCH: The angle of the propeller blade, normally specified in inches theoretically traveled forward during one complete revolution of the propeller.

PITCH: The control movement effected by the elevator causing the aircraft to move in a nose-up or nose-down condition.

PITCHING MOMENT: The displacement up or down, around the longitudinal axis of the fuselage.

PLASTIC SURGEON: One who flies only "ready-to-fly" or "almost-ready-to-fly" planes, of predominately plastic construction.

POLYHEDRAL: Most commonly used on high-performance thermal sailplanes, polyhedral is a dual dihedral break in each wing.

POT: Short for potentiometer, the ceramic, maintenance-free, minute trimming adjustment used for all controls within a transmitter and servo—presently being replaced by solid-state, pre-set devices.

PROP: Abbreviation for propeller.

PROPORTIONAL: Referring to proportional control systems wherein the movement of the control surface is proportional to the amount of movement of the control stick on the transmitter.

PULSE: Referring to an on-off radio transmission.

PUSH ROD: A device designed to transfer the action of an electro-mechanical servo to a given control surface.

PYLON: Pylons are used in pylon racing and are the markers which outline the course around which the pylon racer must fly. (Also see Goodyear.)

RADIAL: Referring to a radial mount wherein the engine is bolted to a plate which, in turn, is bolted against the firewall.

RCVR: Normally used abbreviation for receiver.

RECEIVER-DECODER: That portion of a proportional control system, contained in the R/C plane, which receives the transmitted signal, then decodes the signal and passes it on to the appropriate electro-mechanical servo.

REED: Normally used to refer to the forerunner of today's proportional systems, the "reed" radio, whereby a full-on or full-off signal was triggered by the opening or closing of one or more reed relays.

RESOLUTION: How well a servo follows the stick.

RETRACTABLE LANDING GEAR: Landing gear that is capable of retracting into the wing or fuselage while the model is in flight by means of an electro-mechanical device controlled by the R/C'er at the transmitter.

RETRACTS: A retractible landing gear system.

RF: Radio frequency.

RIB STATIONS: The location of the ribs on the wing plan form.

ROG: Rise-off-ground.

ROLL: The mode of travel affected by the ailerons causing one or the other wing panels to dip, putting the aircraft into a roll or banked condition.

ROTATE: Wrongly used, but refers to the angle of climb on takeoff, or the takeoff itself. (Normally associated with jet flight.)

RPM: Abbreviation indicating revolutions per minute.

RUBBER DUCK: Plastic ready-to-fly, or almost-ready-to-fly plane.

RUDDER: The movable portion of the vertical fin which effects the yaw mode of the aircraft.

RUDDER-ONLY: A simple radio-controlled model which utilizes control of the rudder only.

RUDDERVATOR: A V-shaped control surface which replaces the normal horizontal and vertical stabilizer and which gives both rudder and elevator action to control the yaw and pitch axis of the aircraft.

RUN-IN: Same as break-in, the initial running of an engine so that it reaches an optimum performance potential.

RUNWAY: A strip of ground from which an R/C aircraft can take off.

SAG: An engine on a hot day is subject to heat and humidity and the resulting loss of efficiency is called "sag."

SCALE MODEL: A miniature radio-controlled replica of a full-size aircraft.

SCALE NUT: One devoted to building and flying only copies of full-size planes.

SCALING-DOWN: The reduction of a drawing to a desired size.

SCALING-UP: The enlarging of a drawing to a desired size.

SCOPE: Refers to an oscilloscope used by technicians to check frequencies.

SCRATCH-BUILT: Referring to a model that has been designed and built by the individual modeler or built from plans rather than from a kit.

SEIZING: The sudden stopping of an engine due to overheating.

SEMIPNEUMATIC WHEELS: Hollow tires which retain their shape by the stiffness of the material with which they are made.

SEMISCALE: Often called "stand-off" scale; a model which resembles a full-size aircraft in general configuration although not truly to scale.

SERVO: A electromechanical device which converts an electrical signal into mechanical energy to move a control surface on the aircraft.

SHEET BALSA: Balsa wood which has been fabricated into thin sheets or planks from 2 to 6 inches wide, in thickness from $\frac{1}{32}$ to $\frac{3}{4}$ inch thick, and either 36 or 48 inches in length.

SHOULDER-WING: A model wherein no cabin is used and the wing is mounted directly on top of the fuselage.

SILICONE: A chemical which takes many forms from its use as a lubricant to its use in caulking and adhesive compounds.

SILICONE CARBIDE: A type of wet-or-dry sandpaper.

SILKSPAN: A lightweight covering material that is heavier than Japanese tissue but lighter than silk and is water shrinkable.

SIMPLE CURVE: A surface that curves in one direction only.

SINGLE CHANNEL: A simple type of radio control system which operates on one channel only and is designed to operate one function only, such as the rudder of the aircraft.

SLIP: The term used for "side slip," a prelanding position of the plane where side area of the fuselage is put to work to slow the forward motion of the plane. One definitely *not* for beginners.

SLOP: Looseness of hinges or control rods that allow surfaces to move of their own free will.

SNAP LINK: (Quick-link) clevis pins that attach push rod to control horn or servo.

SPAR: The main longitudinal structural member of the wing, one or more of which are located parallel to the leading edge and the trailing edge of the wing.

SPINNER: The cone-shaped fairing placed over the propeller and attached to the crankshaft of the engine for streamlining purposes.

SPOILERS: Panels hinged to the upper surface of a wing which spoil the lift of the air traveling across the wing, thus causing the plane to descend.

SPORT AIRCRAFT: An R/C model intended primarily for noncompetitive flying.

SPRAY BAR: The tube in the venturi of the engine into which the needle valve is inserted and from which fuel passes into the engine.

STAB: Short for stabilizer.

STABILIZER: The horizontal tail plane.

STATIC THRUST: The pulling power of the engine when the engine is held stationary.

STEERABLE NOSEGEAR: On a tricycle-geared aircraft, the nosegear is often hooked to the rudder servo by means of a push rod in order to afford ground steering capabilities.

STEERING ARM: A control arm mounted on a steerable nose wheel that acts as a tiller in controlling the direction of the aircraft on the ground.

STICK: A movable portion of the transmitter which is manually deflected to transmit a command to the receiver-decoder in the aircraft.

STICK MODE: Referring to the transmitter stick configuration of a given transmitter such as Mode I, Mode II, or Single Stick.

STREAMER: A strip of tissue towed at the end of a line behind an R/C model which an opponent model attempts to cut with his propeller or wing.

STRINGERS: Secondary longitudinal structural members of a fuselage.

STRIP AILERONS: Narrow ailerons attached to the trailing edge of the wing which run almost full span of each panel.

STRIP BALSA: Balsa cut in rectangular cross sections in varying dimensions and lengths of 36 and 48 inches.

SUB-RUDDER: A portion of the rudder which is located beneath the fuselage.

SUPERHET: Referring to a superheterodyne receiver.

SYMMETRICAL AIRFOIL: An airfoil which is identical above and below the centerline of the foil.

TACK: For example, "low-tack," referring to a masking tape used in painting that has minimum adhesion qualities. Or, "tack-cloth"—a rag that has been saturated with a material designed to pick up dust on a model prior to painting.

TAIL MOMENT: The distance from the center of gravity to the rear end of the model.

TE: Trailing edge, referring to the trailing edge of the wing of an aircraft.

TEMPLATE: A pattern used to fabricate aircraft parts.

THERMAL: A rising column of warm air.

THREE-VIEW DRAWING: A set of drawings that presents the side view, front view, and top view of an aircraft.

THROTTLE: That portion of an R/C engine which varies the rpm of the engine through its speed range from idle to full rpm.

THROW: The travel of a control surface or servo.

THRUST ANGLE: The angle between the thrust line and the direction of flight.

THRUST SHIMS: A small wedge-shaped piece of material to alter the thrust line of the engine up or down.

THRUST WEDGES: The same as "thrust shims"; homemade or commercial wedge-shaped pieces of material used to alter the thrust line of an engine and mounted between the engine mounting lugs and the beam motor mounts.

TIP: Referring to the tip of a wing.

TOLEDO: An annual midwinter get-together of R/C enthusiasts in Toledo, Ohio, to see the latest from manufacturers, as well as other enthusiasts' building efforts.

TORQUE: The force of a spinning propeller creating a twisting effect on an airplane in flight. This twist is normally to the left and up, hence the use of right and down engine thrust settings to offset this pull of torque and make the plane fly straight and level until you give it a control that calls for something else.

TOTALED: Memorial services. Plan new plane.

TOW HOOK: A small L-shaped hook which may be either fixed or adjustable, located on the bottom of a sailplane, enabling it to be towed aloft by an electric winch or Hi-Start.

TOW-WINCH: A gasoline- or electric-powered winch used for launching radio-controlled sailplanes.

TRANSMITTER: The hand-held portion of a control system which transmits the command of the operator to the receiver-decoder in the aircraft.

TRICYCLE GEAR: Used to indicate an aircraft with main gear and a steerable or fixed nosegear.

TRIKE: Tricycle (trike) landing gear.

TRIM: The proper adjustment and balance of a model.

TRIM FLIGHTS: The initial flights of a model wherein the model is trimmed for proper flight attitudes.

TRUE WING: A wing that has been built on a flat surface and, when finished, does not have any unwanted twists or warps.

TRUNION BLOCK: A slotted hardwood block used in low-wing aircraft to which the landing gear wire is mounted.

TURBULATOR: A device such as a long thread attached to the wing of a sailplane theoretically to improve the airflow.

TWIN: A two-engined plane.

TWIN GEAR: Two-wheeled landing gear.

UP-ELEVATOR: The deflection of the elevator surface to the upward position causing the plane to change its pitch mode.

UP-WIND: Flying in the direction from which the wind is coming.

VENTURI: The intake portion of the carburetor on a model aircraft engine.

VIBRATION: Any form of vibration that affects a plane's performance, from engine and unbalanced prop vibration to control surface vibration due to loose hinges.

VTO: Vertical takeoff.

WASH-IN: Where the trailing edge of the wing at the tips is twisted slightly downward.

WASH-OUT: Where the trailing edge of the wing at the tips is twisted slightly upward.

WEB: Normally used to indicate lengths of vertically grained balsa glued to the upper and lower spars between the wing ribs to provide torsional rigidity to the wing.

WET SANDING: A process of sanding a painted surface using fine wet-or-dry sandpaper and water.

WHEEL COLLAR: Small metal "donut" with self-contained set screw that slips onto wire of landing gear to hold wheel in place.

WHEEL PANTS: A wheel housing which is normally used to create a streamlined flow of air over the aircraft's wheels.

WIND DRIFT: The movement of an aircraft away from the flyer or intended direction of flight due to wind.

WING AREA: The square inches of a wing, determined by multiplying the span of a wing by its width, e.g., 56-inch span × a 10-inch cord, equals a wing area of 560 square inches.

WING LOADING: A mathematical formula arrived at by dividing the number of square feet of wing area into the total number of ounces of aircraft weight; e.g., wing area is 560 square inches, or 3.88 square feet ($560 \div 144 = 3.88$ square feet). The plane weighs 4½ pounds, or 72 ounces ($72 \div 3.88 = 18$½ ounces per square foot—the wing-loading).

WING RIBS: Formers used in wing construction that determine the airfoil shape.

WINGSPAN: The distance from one tip of the wing to the other tip of the wing as measured on a flat surface.

XMTR: Shorthand for transmitter.

YAW: The movement of the aircraft caused by the rudder, a flat movement of the aft section of the fuselage to the right or left.

APPENDIX

There are many little tricks used in building and maintenance that do not fall under the normal straightforward building or maintenance procedures. To list a few:

WARPS. These normally occur due to the stress of covering, building mistakes, humidity, and the like. To remove warps in wings or stabilizers, hold them over a stove, *taking care not to get too close,* and while moving the warped panel to avoid burning, twist the panel in the direction opposite of the warp. Holding the panel in the twisted position, take it away from the heat and hold it for a minute or two, still twisted. If the warp is one built into the panel it will return in time and the heat treatment must then be repeated. If the warp is due to covering, and this applies only to silk or similar materials with their tremendous shrinking abilities, then the warp may return and again have to be removed with the aid of heat.

MONOKOTE, SOLARFILM. As more and more modelers swing over to these easy-to-use coverings, many complain about these materials sagging after being on the plane for a short while. To prevent this, the plane's frame should be thoroughly dried before covering is begun. Balsa is a highly porous wood, and as such it easily absorbs moisture which makes it enlarge. When the covering is placed over this enlarged wood, the moisture is trapped beneath. As the wood dries under the covering it shrinks and leaves the covering to sag. Drying the frame to prevent this is a simple matter of heating it with a heat gun or passing an iron (on the "wool" setting) over it very slowly. Don't do this on a wet day, and *do* get the covering on as soon as possible after this drying process.

BUBBLES IN COVERING. This is not a common occurrence with MonoKote or Solarfilm, but it can happen. To get rid of the bubbles if they occur, puncture the bubbles with a pin and heat the area again. Bubbles often occur in the trim material used on MonoKote or Solarfilm and the same method is used here too. Stubborn bubbles can be removed by making a small slice with a sharp razor blade and applying heat. If the trim material "smears" due to the heat, use acetone to remove the smeared color. The trim material·and the covering materials are impervious to acetone, so have no fear of harming either.

NOXIOUS ODORS. While many modelers prefer to use the dope and silk method of covering, many people around them cannot stand the smell of dope or thinner. To make dope, acetone, and any glow engine fuel more pleasant, add a few drops of oil of wintergreen or oil of mint, with wintergreen being the more effective of the two (available from drugstores).

PAINTING PLASTIC PARTS. For the modeler who chooses to buy an almost-ready-to-fly (ARF) plane with a plastic fuselage or wing panels, he should be well aware that all paints and plastics are *not* compatible. If no instructions for painting are included with the plane, the modeler should make some tests with various paints *inside* the fuselage. Chances are that an enamel will be the safest choice and that aircraft dope will not work on any plastic. Between these two extremes lie the acrylic and epoxy paints. Spray cans offer the slickest method of application, and for utter beauty a final rubdown with rubbing compound is almost a necessity. However, beware of rubbing compound and enamel. They do not go well together unless the enamel is thoroughly dry, and this may take many weeks. Before attacking a painted finish with rubbing compound, try it on a test panel, and not your painted plane. Any plastic part, regardless of the material from which it is made, should be first washed with detergent before any finishing it attempted.

NYLON PROPS. Although these are only safe on engines up to .29 size, and should be boiled for 30 minutes and cooled in the water used to boil them, they may also be colored to suit a modeler's whim by adding regular fabric dye to the boiling water. A word of caution— if you choose to dye the prop some dark color, plan to paint yellow or white tips on the prop before putting it on your engine. Dark-color props, revolving at 12,000-plus rpm, "disappear," and many a modeler has learned too late that this visibility factor is very important in saving one's fingers and hands from nasty cuts.

STRIPES. For those who are "all thumbs" but want a bit of striping on their creations, I recommend the use of colored drafting or chart tape, available in many widths and colors. These tapes are easy to apply and solve the problem for those less than proficient with brush and paint. These tapes may also be used to mark off doors, windows, or nonworking control surfaces, as well as brace lines on windows and windshields.

FCC RADIO LICENSE. Although R/C is called by some a "license-free" activity, don't let the word "free" fool you. You must have an FCC license in your possession when operating your equipment. "Free," as used in this case, means exam-free. The license costs $20 for five years, but many AMA clubs carry a club license that covers all members. Be sure to check on this when joining a club to be certain you are operating your equipment legally. Inspectors make spot checks, and if you're caught without a license the penalties involved are far more expensive than the price of the license.

WOOD SELECTION. Should you need to purchase wood to replace bad parts in a kit, or you choose to use a set of plans and buy all the wood to build the plane, choose the wood carefully—each section of construction requires a different type of wood.

There are three cuts made in a balsa log (see page 70). Each cut gives a different type of grain, and therefore strength. "A" grain is the "softest," or most easily bendable, and is used to sheet leading edges of wings and other places where wood must assume a curvature. "B" grain is a bit stiffer and is used to plank fuselages, make wing ribs and body formers, and so on. "C" grain wood is stiff and quite difficult to bend across its width; it is used for longerons, uprights, spars, and similar members. C grain is also used for wing ribs by many builders because of its stiffness, and if light enough C grain wood can be found, it is ideal for solid stabilizers and rudders because it does not warp as easily as A and B grain stock, even though B grain is normally adequate for rudder and stabilizer, and tends to be lighter than C grain.

PUBLICATIONS. R/C is a fast-changing hobby, and in order to keep up with all the new developments you will want to subscribe to one or more of the magazines devoted in whole or part to the sport. These are:

American Aircraft Modeler
733 15th St. N.W.
Washington, D.C. 20005

R/C Modeler Magazine
171 West Sierra Madre Blvd.
Sierra Madre, California 91024

Flying Models
31 Arch St.
Ramsey, New Jersey 07446

The Model Builder
12552 Del Rey Dr.
Santa Ana, California 92705

Model Airplane News
1 North Broadway
White Plains, New York 10601

While all these magazines try to maintain a system of complete national distribution, it doesn't always work. If you cannot find them at your newsstand, write to them at the addresses shown and ask for yearly subscription rates. One is devoted entirely to R/C, but all carry heavy R/C coverage of varying nature. Only *you* can decide which you will wish to have as monthly reading material. (Roughly 75 percent of the R/C enthusiasts subscribe to *all* the publications.)

BUY FOR LESS. Few but the absolute novices pay full price for their hobby materials. Most hobby shops in the United States offer a "club discount," another valuable reason for belonging to an organized club. Unless you are one of the more affluent citizens to whom savings mean little, a club membership can often save you a great deal over a yearly period.

PLYWOOD. When building a R/C plane, use only "aircraft grade" plywood, material that consists of *five plys* of securely bonded wood layers. The use of household type plywood will result in little but disaster when this inferior product shakes apart due to vibration working on its low-quality component adhesion. The high-quality plywood is available in sizes from $\frac{1}{64}$-inch thickness to over $\frac{1}{4}$-inch thickness, and while it may seem expensive, it's cheap in view of its sensational strength and insurance of holding to protect your aircraft and radio gear.

"CHINA MARKER". A china marker is a black crayon in a paper-wrap casing and you can find one in any stationery store and in many hardware stores. (It is also available in red and white.) These are used to mark Solarfilm and MonoKote for cutting to exact patterns, or to mark specific positions on either material—such as hinge locations, push-rod exits, and similar details.

A china marker is also good on many other seemingly unmarkable surfaces, such as metal and the celluloid used for canopies or windshields. To remove the markings after their need has been fulfilled, wipe them away with a tissue dampened with alcohol or lighter fluid.

WINDSHIELDS—CANOPIES. Sticking these in place stumps many a beginner. It's all done quite easily with Pliobond or a similar type of contact cement, using a small brush (NOT the one in the bottle!) to lay a thin bead of cement on the canopy or windshield, and another thin bead where both are to fit on the model. Allowing 15 minutes for drying of both cement coated surfaces, the two are very carefully joined to each other. Covering the cemented areas is accomplished with draftsman's tape, available in many colors (and metallic finishes) from art and drafting supply stores, as well as a good number of hobby shops.

CLOSING NOTE

Many of the drawings and photos in this book came from *R/C Modeler Magazine* and its book, *R/C Modeler Flight Training Course*. The book goes into deeper detail than this one and is therefore a perfect follow-up to the material presented herein. In closing, my deepest thanks go to Pat Crews and Don Dewey of *R/CM* for their instant cooperation in supplying the material I requested for this publication.

ROBERT LOPSHIRE

INDEX